Christopher Geering has been practising in Professional Discipline for over fifteen years and is ranked Band 1 by Chambers and Partners in this area. He appears for professionals before a wide variety of tribunals, as well as assisting with judicial review and appeal proceedings in the High Court. He lives in Blackheath with his wife and two girls.

A Practical Guide to Fitness to Practise Proceedings Before Healthcare Regulators

A Practical Guide to Fitness to Practise Proceedings Before Healthcare Regulators

Christopher Geering

Barrister

2 Hare Court

Law Brief Publishing

Published 2026 by Law Brief Publishing, an imprint of Law Brief Publishing Ltd
30 The Parks
Minehead
Somerset
TA24 8BT

www.lawbriefpublishing.com

Paperback: 978-1-918241-29-7

To my wife, Helen, who I met at the NMC,
and who brightens up my world.

PREFACE

The importance of healthcare regulation cannot be overstated. On the one hand, Regulators aim to protect the public from harm, on the other their decisions can also destroy the livelihoods and reputations of their members.

In recognition of this importance, an increasing number of lawyers now specialise in Fitness to Practise proceedings. This book is an accessible introduction to the main procedural practices and legal principles by which professionals are judged and on which their careers often depend. It guides the practitioner through the minutiae of healthcare regulation, including interim orders, substantive hearings, review hearings and appeals. It is ideal for lawyers starting out in this area, but also provides a handy and manageable aide memoire of the key issues and cases for those experienced in such work.

The law stated in this book is believed to be accurate and up to date as at 1st March 2026.

Christopher Geering
March 2026

CONTENTS

CHAPTER ONE

INTRODUCTION

Scope

This book is intended as an introduction to assist advocates appearing for the first time before healthcare regulators in fitness to practise (FTP) proceedings – that is to say, in proceedings seeking to limit or remove a professional's registration with their regulator. It does not seek to apply these principles to other regulatory environments, although of course there will be considerable cross-over.

I stress this is an introduction only. For a compendious summary of the relevant caselaw, I thoroughly recommend investing in a copy of Kenneth Hamer's "Professional Conduct Casebook".

It is important to be clear at the outset there is no uniform or unified FTP process across healthcare regulators. Each regulator is governed by its own legislation, rules and guidance. The General Medical Council (GMC) FTP regime, for example, is underpinned by the Medical Act 1983. It is also governed by its Fitness to Practise rules, which are set out in a statutory instrument. A tribunal will also have regard to various forms of guidance issued by the GMC – e.g. its sanction policy, its interim orders guidance etc. Much of these sources of law and guidance will be substantially similar to those governing the General Dental Council (GDC), Nursing and Midwifery Council (NMC), Social Work England (SWE) etc. However, there are also significant differences in procedure and practice. By way of example, in a typical case most regulators require a tribunal to determine the facts, decide if these amount to misconduct, consider if the registrant is currently impaired, and – if so – issue the appropriate sanction. However, not all do. The General Chiropractic Council (GCC) and General Osteopathic Council (GOsC) have no separate impairment stage.

Nonetheless, each healthcare regime shares broadly the same features and process. They borrow heavily from each other's procedures, and rely extensively upon each other's caselaw. Of note, they are all subject to the same oversight by the Professional Standards Authority – the "regulator of regulators" – which can challenge their decisions in the High Court if they are insufficient to protect the public.

In respect of terminology, a member of a healthcare profession is generally referred to as a "*registrant*" – I have done so already. Regulators perform several different roles. In the context of FTP, each regulator will both investigate complaints and – through its FTP committees / panels / tribunals – adjudicate upon them. These functions are performed by separate departments within the same regulatory body. To emphasis this distinction, the GMC rebranded its adjudicating functions as the Medical Practitioners Tribunal Service (MPTS). This is operationally independent of the GMC but has no separate legislative existence. Other regulators have followed suit – the GDC's adjudicating function is now referred to as the Dental Professionals Hearing Service (DPHS). Not all bodies have formalised the separation in the same way.

Civil proceedings?

It is not my intention to set out any kind of potted history to FTP proceedings. However, it is right to say that for a long time FTP proceedings were considered quasi-criminal in nature. Not least, determinations were made to the criminal standard. The position has shifted markedly over the years. The standard of proof is now the civil standard across all healthcare regulators. The courts also have expressly commented that proceedings are civil in nature – e.g. R (Kuzmin) v General Medical Council [2019] EWHC 2129 (Admin).

Nonetheless, FTP proceedings still draw heavily upon elements of criminal law. Any application for abuse of process, or to exclude hearsay evidence, or to stop a case at half time are likely to be rooted in principles drawn from the criminal law. The format of the FTP process shares few of the mutual disclosure obligations we see in civil proceedings. By this I mean, in general, the registrant cannot be compelled to provide documents which may assist the regulator. Rather, the regulator sets out charges it wishes to bring against the registrant, and the registrant defends themselves in much the same way as in a criminal trial. Moreover, there is limited scope for any form of settlement, and – as a rule – costs do not simply follow the event.

In short, without taking anything away from the court's repetition that these are civil proceedings, it is important to appreciate they have their own procedure and character, and much of this has a basis in criminal law.

Process

In general, most FTP processes follow the same basic pattern –

A concern (referral) is submitted to the regulator alleging a professional is not fit to practise. This referral must be relevant to one or more of the statutory grounds for finding the registrant impaired. Each Act sets out these bases for impairment in slightly different ways. However, these are commonly misconduct, deficient professional performance, health or criminal conviction.

Regulators have screening processes to discard those referrals which are not potentially relevant to a registrant's fitness to practise. Assuming a referral is not screened off, the regulator will commission an investigation to gather evidence. This investigation, and any response from the registrant, will be considered by the Case Examiners or Investigating Committee, depending on the organisation.

The Case Examiners / Investigating Committee sit in private and consider on the papers whether there is a realistic prospect of the facts being proved, and – if so – if there is a realistic prospect of a finding of impairment. If these tests are met the case is likely to be sent to a final hearing.

Certain regulators allow their Case Examiners broader powers – for example, to offer warnings or to suggest agreed undertakings to avoid a case otherwise going to a hearing. Since the focus of this book is the hearing process itself, I do not propose to go into these alternative disposals.

At the final hearing the registrant will face an allegation that their fitness to practise is impaired on the bases of one or more of the statutory grounds. The Notice of Hearing will set out the factual allegations, and allege that as a result of these acts the registrant is impaired by reason of misconduct etc.

The Tribunal must consider:

(i) are the facts proved,

(ii) if so, do any of them amount to the statutory ground of impairment pleaded (e.g. misconduct),

(iii) if so, is the registrant still impaired as a result,

(iv) if so, what sanction is appropriate.

This reference to current impairment will be dealt with in depth in due course. Essentially it means: should there be some kind of restriction to protect the public or the reputation of the profession.

Typically (i) is called the facts stage. Once this is concluded and announced most tribunals will hear evidence and submissions on (ii) and (iii). This is the impairment stage. Once this decision is announced, (iv) is the sanction stage.

There is, as always, some variation. As noted already, some regulators like the GOsC and GCC have no impairment stage. The General Optical Council (GOC) separate out misconduct and impairment into separate stages. The GDC hear stages (ii)-(iv) together.

As an example of how a case may operate in practice, I will consider a (slightly contrived) example. Dr Smith is alleged to have sexually assaulted a patient and to have kept poor records. The allegation may be set out like this:

> *"It is alleged that Dr Smith, on or around 1 December 2023:*
>
> 1. *Touched Patient A's breast:*
>   a. *Without her consent*
>   b. *Without clinical justification;*
> 2. *His actions at 1 above were sexually motivated;*
> 3. *Failed to keep accurate records of this appointment.*
>
> *And his fitness to practise is impaired by reason of misconduct"*

The hearing would broadly work like this:

Facts stage: the tribunal has to consider whether the factual particulars are proved. Each must be proved to the civil standard. It hears evidence and submissions from both parties in the usual way. It goes into private to make a decision. It then moves back into public session and announces its decision. In this example the facts are all proved.

Impairment stage: the representatives make submissions on the issue of both misconduct and impairment. In private the tribunal first consider whether any of those facts amount to misconduct. In this case the tribunal finds 1 and 2 constitute misconduct but 3 does not. The tribunal will then move on to consider, in light of 1 and 2 only, whether Dr Smith's practise is currently impaired. The tribunal considers that it is. It returns to public session and announces its decision on misconduct and impairment.

Sanction stage: the parties make further submissions. The tribunal then retires to decide what sanction is appropriate. This is announced in public.

Barring the need for an interim / immediate order (which I will deal with in due course) or very exceptionally an application for costs, that is the end of the process.

Importantly at each stage the tribunal provides reasons.

Tribunal

The terminology differs across regulators – panel / committee / tribunal. There is nothing significant in this choice of name.

When a case goes to a final hearing, or an interim hearing, each regulator requires that a tribunal includes a mixture of both lay and professional experience. In other words, for a nursing case at least one member of the tribunal must be a nurse, and at least one must not be.

It used to be the rule that most tribunals would comprise three members, and they would be assisted by advice from an independent legal assessor who would not participate in the decision-making process. Certain regulators have moved away from this model (e.g. GMC, General Pharmaceutical Council (GPhC) and now have a legally qualified chair, a registrant member and a third member (lay or professional). In such cases there is no need for an independent legal assessor.

Some regulators use tribunals with five members (GOC), but most use three. However they are constituted, the common feature is this: they <u>all</u> include experience from within the profession and outside it.

Adversarial or inquisitorial?

There is an important distinction between an FTP panel and a judge considering a case at first instance. The High Court in <u>Ruscillo v Council</u>

for the Regulation of Health Care Professionals [2004] Ewca Civ 1356 commented,

> "*The disciplinary tribunal should play a more proactive role than a judge presiding over a criminal trial in making sure that the case is properly presented and that the relevant evidence is placed before it.*" [para 80]

Therefore, as PSA v General Medical Council and Lingam [2023] EWHC 967 (Admin) put it, "*an inquisitorial duty falls upon a Panel hearing a professional regulatory matter in the public interest*" [para 16]. Mostyn J went further in Towuaghantse v General Medical Council [2021] EWHC 681 (Admin) when he said "*Regulatory proceedings of the type with which I am concerned are quintessentially inquisitorial.*" [para 31]

In my view that puts the position too strongly. Coronial proceedings are "*quintessentially inquisitorial*" – the coroner decides what evidence to call, leads on the questioning of witnesses, and there is no scope for advocates to make submissions on what evidence should be preferred or rejected. FTP proceedings still operate in the usual adversarial way in most regards. Not least, the prosecutor, not the tribunal, lead on the questioning of their witnesses.

However, tribunals can and do question witnesses after both parties have had their chance to do so. The tribunal can amend particulars of the allegation on its own initiative. It has a duty to ensure a case is not under-prosecuted, and can even add a further particular of charge, if appropriate. It can compel the prosecution to call a witness or produce a document. These powers are discussed in Professional Standards Authority v (1) Nursing and Midwifery Council and (2) Jozi [2015] EWHC 764 (Admin). In that sense, it is inquisitorial. However, in reality, it is comparatively rare for tribunals to adopt such an interventionalist approach.

CHAPTER TWO

PRELIMINARIES

Proceeding in absence

Registrants will often not engage in proceedings. Regulators' FTP rules contain express provision for hearings to proceed in the absence of the registrant. Once it can be shown the regulator has sent the registrant the Notice of the Hearing in the appropriate form, the question is then whether it is in the interests of justice for the case to proceed in their absence.

The House of Lords' judgment in R v Jones [2001] EWCA Crim 168 provides relevant guidance, which is frequently relied on. The decision whether to proceed in absence should be made with caution. The court provides several factors to consider, including:

- Has the registrant absented themselves voluntarily?
- Would an adjournment result in their attendance?
- The extent of their disadvantage if the hearing proceeded without them.
- The length of any such adjournment.
- The effect of delay on witnesses' memories.
- The public interest in trials being conducted in a reasonable time frame.

The Court of Appeal in Adeogba v GMC [2016] EWCA Civ 162 noted the parallel with criminal proceedings cannot be taken too far, not least because in FTP proceedings the prosecution cannot have practitioners arrested and brought to court. The court summed up the position succinctly:

> "*It would run entirely counter to the protection, promotion and maintenance of the health and safety of the public if a practitioner could effectively frustrate the process and challenge a refusal to adjourn when that practitioner had deliberately failed to engage in the process. The consequential cost and delay to other cases is real. Where there is good reason not to proceed, the case should be adjourned; where there is not, however, it is only right that it should proceed.*" [para 19]

There is an onus on professionals who are subject to a regulatory regime to engage with the regulator: "*That is part of the responsibility to which they sign up when being admitted to the profession.*" [para 20]

So, to take an example, if a registrant is unaware of an FTP hearing because they have not provided the GMC with up-to-date contact information, it is likely the hearing will proceed in their absence. The process cannot be frustrated by a practitioner neglecting their duty to the regulator.

Jones and Adeogba do not deal with one relevant feature. It seems to me the nature of the hearing in question is highly relevant when deciding whether it is fair to proceed in absence. If a final hearing proceeds in absence it may well make adverse findings of fact and impose a sanction which can only be challenged by way of appeal. The same is not true of an interim order, which makes no factual findings, and can potentially be reviewed and removed without recourse to the High Court.

Often a registrant will rely on medical evidence to explain their lack of attendance or to request an adjournment. As per Adeogba the onus is on the registrant to provide sufficient evidence to support this position.

In General Medical Council v Hayat [2018] EWCA Civ 2796 the Court of Appeal noted that where a medical condition was put forward as justification for an adjournment, there must be evidence "*the individual is unfit to participate in the hearing... That evidence must identify with proper particularity the individual's condition and explain why that condition prevents their participation in the hearing.*" [para 37]

The court quoted the test in Levy v Ellis-Carr [2012] EWCA Civ 2796:

> *"In my judgment... such evidence should identify the medical attendant and give details of his familiarity with the party's medical condition (detailing all recent consultations), should identify with particularity what the patient's medical condition is and the features of that condition which (in the medical attendant's opinion) prevent participation in the trial process, should provide a reasoned prognosis and should give the court some confidence that what is being expressed is an independent opinion after a proper examination. It is being tendered as expert evidence. The court can then consider what weight to attach to that opinion, and what arrangements might be made (short of an adjournment) to accommodate a party's difficulties. No judge is bound to accept expert evidence"* [para 36]

If inadequate medical evidence is served, there is no duty on the tribunal to make further inquiries.

These prescriptions cannot be taken too far. When dealing with interim order hearings, for example, the short notice provided may preclude detailed medical evidence being available. Moreover, a condition may develop the day before the hearing. However, the general point remains: the burden is on the registrant to obtain sufficient evidence to explain their absence, or request for an adjournment.

If a case does proceed in the absence of the registrant, it is important to ensure the proceedings are as fair as possible. In Sanusi v General Medical Council [2019] EWCA Civ 1172 there was relevant mitigation material in the GMC's possession which should have been provided to the tribunal:

> *"(A)s a matter of natural justice and fairness, both the General Medical Council and a Medical Practitioners Tribunal dealing with a case of serious misconduct should take reasonable steps to ensure that all relevant mitigation material provided by an absent registrant is available for consideration by the panel when it comes to deal with sanction. That obligation is not however unlimited. It does not require extensive trawls through the archives, nor extend to sifting through large quantities of unindexed or uncategorised documentation provided by a registrant to determine what if any relevance it may have. The obligation extends only to reasonable searches for material that is objectively viewed as relevant."* [para 84]

This principle is not unique to the sanction stage of proceedings. If a case proceeds in absence, the regulator should consider whether in fairness to the registrant particular documents / information in their possession should be provided to the tribunal.

As for the role of the tribunal, in McDaid v NMC [2013] EWHC 586 (Admin) the court observed:

> *"if the Panel does decide to proceed in the absence of the defendant, it seems to me vital that it performs its tasks properly and not merely as part of a rubber-stamping exercise… (T)he Panel was required during the giving of evidence by the NMC witnesses to take reasonable steps to expose weaknesses in the NMC case and to make such points on behalf of the Defendant as the evidence permitted.*
>
> *However, it is important to note that the test… does not suggest that there is any duty on the Panel to cross-examine witnesses in the way that such exercise might be performed whether by a litigant in person or by any legal representative… (I)t is important to note that the test as formulated only requires the Panel to take "reasonable steps" to expose weaknesses in the case of the opposing party. What such*

> *"reasonable steps" might be will of necessity depend upon the particular circumstances of the particular case in question.*" [para 43]

Public or private?

Most final hearings will be conducted in public – by "final hearing" I mean hearings where the allegations made against a registrant are determined. The position is less clear cut with interim orders.Some regulators like the GMC hear interim orders (see below) in private, unless there is an application for the case to be heard in public. Others, such as the NMC, hear interim orders in public also.

In the case of a public hearing, there is scope for asking for all or part of a hearing to be conducted in private. This is usually on the basis that matters of health need to be ventilated.

Whatever the basis of the application for privacy, the extent of any departure from open justice should be kept to a minimum [A v BBC [2015] AC 588]. It may be that only part of the case will be heard in private, and the rest can proceed in public. In addition, a complainant in a clinical case will usually be referred to as Patient A, for example, so matters of a private nature relating to their treatment may be discussed in open session without the need for the whole case to be heard in private.

A practice has arisen where regulators will not refer to witnesses by their full names in published decisions, but anonymise them as Witness 1, Witness 2 etc without making any such application to the tribunal. The High Court criticised this practice in Lu v SRA [2022] EWHC 1729(Admin):

> "*Courts and tribunals should not be squeamish about naming innocent people caught up in alleged wrongdoing of others. It is part of the price of open justice and there is no presumption that their privacy is more important than open justice.*" [para 138]

Exceptionally, the registrant can ask for anonymity. In doing so it will be of assistance to look at the approach taken in the civil courts under CPR 39.2(4), as set out in XXX v Camden London Borough Council [2020] EWCA Civ 1468. The court noted the following factors which needed to be considered:

- The fundamental importance of open justice, subject to specified exceptions (Scott v Scott [1913] AC 417);

- The court should be careful to prevent extensions to exceptions by analogy (R. v Legal Aid Board Ex p. Kaim Todner [1999] Q.B. 966;)

- Article 2 and 3 ECHR will be engaged if someone is at "*real and immediate risk of death*" or a real risk of inhuman or degrading treatment if their identity is disclosed.

- Article 8 right to privacy is an argument in favour of restrictions. As against that, the common law rights of the public and press to know about court proceedings are also protected by Article 10.

- In S (A child) (Identification: Restrictions on Publication) [2004] UKHL 47, [2005] 1 AC 593 at [17], Lord Steyn stated that when a court considers balancing competing human rights interests, four principles could be identified:

  > "*First, neither article has as such precedence over the other. Second, where the values under the two articles are in conflict, an intense focus on the comparative importance of the specific rights being claimed in the individual case is necessary. Thirdly, the justifications for interfering with or restricting each right must be taken into account. Finally, the proportionality test must be applied to each. For convenience I will call this the ultimate balancing test*"

- It is relevant to consider the extent to which material has, or is about, to become public.

In MXM v General Medical Council [2022] EWHC 817 (Admin) it was alleged the doctor had conducted an affair with a patient. The interim order was challenged in the High Court and the court agreed to anonymise the doctor on the basis of detrimental effect publicity may have on his children:

> "*I determined that, in this case, the article 8 rights of the Applicant and his young children outweigh the article 10 rights of the press and the public in being able to identify him as the Applicant in these proceedings.*
>
> *In evaluating the interference with article 10 rights, I bore in mind the fundamental importance of open justice and the importance of the press interest in the names of parties as explained by Lord Rodger in Re Guardian News and Media Ltd [2010] 2 AC 697 at 723 . I noted the scope of the restriction sought does not inhibit the press or public knowing any of the details of the case, other than identifying details.*
>
> *In evaluating the interference with article 8 rights, I bore in mind the ages of the children which make them particularly vulnerable to being made aware by fellow pupils of the nature of the evidence, if the Applicant were to be identified in the press. I noted the evidence of the detrimental impact on the 16 year old child of being informed of these matters by TR. I assessed that the concerns for the welfare of the children were genuine and well-founded.*"

In GMC v X [2019] EWHC 493 (Admin) Dr X's case was heard in private. He then applied for the decision not to be published, even in a redacted form – only the mere fact he was suspended. His concern was that publication would reveal his sexuality and there was evidence this would give rise to a real risk of suicide. The High Court commented there was a public interest in the GMC's maintenance of a public register and in publishing the tribunal's findings. However, the public interest was not absolute and had to be balanced with the doctor's ECHR rights – here the real risk of X's suicide engaged the doctor's right to life under Article 2. The risk was real and immediate. The High Court concluded, "*in the very particular facts of this case, this risk overwhelms the public interest*". [para 173]

Remote hearing or in person?

Prior to 2020 it was usual for all hearings to be conducted in person. The Covid pandemic caused a massive shift in favour of remote hearings. It is now usual for interim order hearings and procedural hearings to be conducted remotely. In the case of substantive hearings, the position is less clear cut. In general a regulator will want a hearing to proceed remotely, as it presents a significant saving, but is unlikely to contest a registrant's request for an in-person hearing. It is also open to a regulator to agree to a hybrid hearing. It may well be that the need to be in person applies only to the fact-finding stage, for example.

In the event there is no agreement about the form of the hearing, there is considerable guidance on the issue. Much of this arose in the context of the pandemic but these cases remain relevant. As the court observed in Re B (A Child) [2020] EWCA 584: "*the fundamental principles of substantive law and procedural fairness are unchanged... A remote hearing, where it is appropriate, can replicate some but not all of the characteristics of a fully attended hearing*". [para 4]

Remote hearings are less effective at managing hearings with significant witness evidence. In SC v University Hospital Southampton NHS Foundation Trust (Rev 2) [2020] EWHC 1445 (QB) the court noted:

> *"the complex multi-layered human communications and observations that take place during a substantial witness trial are significantly impeded when the hearing is conducted remotely. A video-conference*

is necessarily two-dimensional and permissive only of bilateral communication and observation". [para 26]

The most helpful summary of relevant factors is set out in Re A (Children (Remote Hearing: Care and Placement Orders) [2020] EWCA Civ 583. The Court of Appeal commented:

> *"The factors that are likely to influence the decision on whether to proceed with a remote hearing will vary from case to case, court to court and judge to judge. We consider that they will include*
>
> *i) The importance and nature of the issue to be determined; is the outcome that is sought an interim or final order?*
>
> *ii) Whether there is a special need for urgency, or whether the decision could await a later hearing without causing significant disadvantage to the child or the other parties;*
>
> *iii) Whether the parties are legally represented;*
>
> *iv) The ability, or otherwise, of any lay party… to engage with and follow remote proceedings meaningfully. This factor will include access to and familiarity with the necessary technology, funding, intelligence/personality, language, ability to instruct their lawyers (both before and during the hearing), and other matters;*
>
> *v) Whether evidence is to be heard or whether the case will proceed on the basis of submissions only;*
>
> *vi) The source of any evidence that is to be adduced and assimilated by the court. For example, whether the evidence is written or oral, given by a professional or lay witness, contested or uncontested, or factual or expert evidence;*
>
> *vii) The scope and scale of the proposed hearing. How long is the hearing expected to last?*

viii) The available technology; telephone or video, and if video, which platform is to be used. A telephone hearing is likely to be a less effective medium than using video;

ix) The experience and confidence of the court and those appearing before the court in the conduct of remote hearings using the proposed technology;

x) Any safe (in terms of potential COVID 19 infection) alternatives that may be available for some or all of the participants to take part in the court hearing by physical attendance in a courtroom before the judge or magistrates." [para 9]

CHAPTER THREE

INTERIM ORDERS

Introduction

An interim order is a temporary restriction imposed on a registrant whilst the regulator conducts its investigation and the matter is brought to a final hearing. Each regulator will have some form of interim order guidance, which will assist in preparing for the hearing.

There are two forms of interim order – conditions of practise, or suspension. An interim order of conditions of practice enables the registrant to continue to work subject to particular limitations. An order of suspension means they cannot work as a registrant at all. In effect, they are treated as being off the register.

Interim order hearings are usually conducted remotely. It is possible for live evidence to be called (although permission may be required) but in the overwhelming majority of cases the hearing will be dealt with through submissions. As I have said, some regulators will hear interim order applications in public. Others, such as the GMC, do so in private, as a default position. It will be necessary to check.

The hearing will work in this way typically:

In advance of the hearing the regulator will provide the tribunal with a bundle of evidence. The defence can do likewise. Usually this will comprise references, and evidence of past safe practise.

At the hearing the regulator will explain (i) why an order is necessary to protect the public, or it's otherwise in the public interest, (ii) why an order is proportionate, (iii) why the particular order of conditions or suspension is appropriate, (iv) how long the order should be. The defence will then respond. The legal assessor or legally qualified chair will give advice. The tribunal will then make a decision that day and announce it in public. A written copy of the decision will be provided.

Not fact finding

In general, a regulator may impose an interim order if it is (i) necessary for public protection, (ii) otherwise in the public interest, and/or (iii) in the registrant's own interest. This is the approach before the GMC, GDC and NMC, for example. The GOsC, however, can only impose an interim order on the basis of public protection. Again, it is best to check the particular approach of each regulator.

In considering whether any ground is made out, the tribunal will not make any findings of fact. Rather, it essentially undertakes a risk assessment. There must be some evidence to support the concerns, but the tribunal will not come to a decision as to whether those concerns are proved or not. In Perry v Nursing and Midwifery Council [2013] EWCA 145 the Court of Appeal summarised the tribunal's role in this way:

> "*the Committee must decide whether, on the basis of the allegation and evidence against the registrant, including any admission by him, it is satisfied that an order is necessary for the protection of the public, or otherwise in the public interest or in the interests of the registrant himself. The Committee must of course permit both parties to make their submissions on the need for an interim order and, if one is to be made, its nature and its terms. For that purpose it must consider the nature of the evidence on which the allegation made against the registrant is based. It is entitled to discount evidence that is inconsistent with objective or undisputed evidence or which is manifestly unreliable. The Committee may receive and assess evidence on the effect of an interim order on the registrant, and the registrant is entitled to give evidence on this. The registrant may also give evidence, if he can, to establish that the allegation is manifestly unfounded or manifestly exaggerated; but the Committee is not otherwise required to hear his evidence as to whether or not the*

> *substantive allegation against him is or is not well-founded: that is not the issue on the application for an interim order.*
>
> *What the Committee cannot do, and should not do, is to seek to decide the credibility or merits of a disputed allegation: that is a matter for the substantive hearing… Necessarily, at the interim stage, the Committee must not and cannot decide disputed issues of fact in relation to the substantive allegations. The Committee must also be extremely cautious about rejecting or discounting evidence on the basis that it is incredible or implausible.*" [para 19]

There is one exception to this principle. In White v GMC [2021] EWHC 3286 (Admin) the court considered the appropriateness of an interim order of conditions preventing Dr White publishing his anti-vaccination views. In overturning the order, the court observed that section 12 of the Human Rights Act 1998 provides that where a tribunal is considering whether to grant any relief which might affect the exercise of the right to freedom of speech "*no such relief is to be granted so as to restrain publication before trial unless the court is satisfied that the applicant is likely to establish that publication should not be allowed*".

Some assessment of the prospects of success is, therefore, required in such a case. This is very much a limited exception.

On the face of it, it may be thought there will rarely be a need for a defence advocate to address the factual criticisms made against a registrant since the tribunal is not there to determine the truth or otherwise of those allegations. In reality, there will be occasions when it is worth doing so. If there is evidence which undermines the weight which may otherwise be given to allegations, that should be emphasised.

The grounds for an interim order

An order for public protection may only be imposed if it is "*necessary*". This is taken to denote a high bar. NMC v Persand [2023] EWHC 3356 (Admin) commented:

> *"... in every case, the NMC committee and the Court, has to ask itself precisely why it is said to be "necessary" to impose an interim sanction on the nurse. If the case is that it is necessary to protect patients, then there needs to be an intense focus on how and why the evidence demonstrates that patients may be at risk from the nurse and how serious that risk is...*
>
> *Simply saying that, if a nurse was free to practise without being subject to conditions, such a circumstance would raise concerns in the minds of a member of the public is, in my judgment, wholly insufficient. Equally, saying that there is some limited risk to patients from a nurse's clinical practice if he or she is allowed to continue to practice without restrictions is equally insufficient. It seems to me that the necessity test requires the NMC to show that, on the particular facts of a case, there are features of the case which mean that matters are so serious that it is justifiable to restrain the exercise of professional skills by a nurse at a stage when the allegations are unproven. The test is something close to saying that an interim order is essential, in the sense that a responsible regulator would not be acting properly in failing to act on a proven risk to the public."* [para 41, 45]

The degree of risk, and the extent of harm if the risk were to eventuate, are always relevant considerations. Any assessment of risk will need to be put into the context of all the other evidence available speaking to the registrant's competence or character. It is common for the defence, therefore, to provide character evidence, and evidence of any retraining or reflection.

Usually an order will be sought on the limb of public protection and the public interest. It is relatively rare for an order to be imposed on the public interest limb alone. Shiekh v GDC [2007] EWHC 2972 (Admin) concerned a dentist who was convicted of conspiracy to defraud and a prison sentence of 12 months, suspended for 18 months. A tribunal imposed an interim suspension order in the public interest. The High Court overturned this. In doing so it commented:

> "*the bar is set high; and I think that, in the ordinary case at least, necessity is an appropriate yardstick. That is so because of reasons of proportionality. It is a very serious thing indeed for a dentist or a doctor to be suspended. It is serious in many cases just because of the impact on that person's right to earn a living. It is serious in all cases because of the detriment to him in reputational terms. Accordingly, it is, in my view, likely to be a relatively rare case where a suspension order will be made on an interim basis on the ground that it is in the public interest.*
>
> ...
>
> *The difficulty I have in this particular case is trying to get a purchase on why it was that each Panel thought that interim suspension was needed. This was not a case of ongoing or future risk or anything like that. Many of the points that the Panel made might well have been apposite... if one was considering at the final hearing why suspension was needed. But what is difficult to grasp, certainly from the reasons that were given by the Panels so far as there were reasons, is their assessment that suspension was needed on an interim basis. If it is to be the case that the justification was that of public perception and public confidence, then one might have thought that that could be reflected by an appropriate decision by the Panel, if so minded, at the final hearing when all the facts had been fully explored*" [para 16, 23]

When such an application is made on this ground alone, it is, therefore, highly relevant to stress that the public interest will be vindicated at the final hearing if the allegation is in fact proved, and to ask what special features in the instant case warrant an additional restriction at the interim stage? In doing so, as noted above, it should be stressed that Sheikh concerned a criminal conviction for dishonesty, and a custodial sentence (albeit suspended).

Nonetheless, there clearly are cases where such an order is appropriate on this limb alone. Where the doctor is being investigated for serious criminality unconnected with their work, especially sexual offences, the regulator will often contend that the public would be shocked if the doctor was able to carry on working pending a final hearing. D v GMC [2015] EWHC 847 (Admin) concerned a GP accused of blackmailing his ex-girlfriend foraround £90,000 in return for not distributing photos of her. Lang J upheld his interim suspension:

> "*I consider that a properly informed and reasonable member of the public would be surprised and dismayed to learn that his or her treating doctor was awaiting a Crown Court trial on this serious charge, which would potentially lead to imprisonment and erasure, and yet the regulator had permitted him to practise, without informing his patients....In my view, this is one of those rare cases in which the serious nature of the allegations means that there is a real likelihood of serious damage to public confidence in the profession if the Claimant is allowed to continue to practise pending trial, even though he may yet be acquitted. In those circumstances, I conclude that it was in the public interest for an interim order of suspension to be made, and the Panel was right to do so.*" [para 42]

As a general rule, the "*otherwise in the registrant's interests*" is only deployed in health cases where the registrant really needs to manage an addiction / health condition before returning to the workplace. To my knowledge an interim order has never been imposed on this basis alone. In such a case it would be strange for an order to be needed on this basis alone where there was not also a public protection issue as well.

Conditions or suspensions

If any ground for an interim order is established, the tribunal must then consider if an interim conditions of practice order will address the risk identified. Only if it will not, should a tribunal move on to an interim suspension order.

Regulators will usually have a conditions "bank" for tribunals to consider. These set out various different conditions, which may be appropriate in particular cases. However, the tribunal is not bound by these. It can adapt them as it sees fit, or formulate conditions which are not in the bank at all.

Each condition must be necessary. Persand observed: "*the test of "necessity" applies just as much to each individual condition imposed on a nurse as it does to any case of suspension. I thus have to ask whether each of the conditions satisfies that test.*" [para 47]

The conditions must, therefore, be linked to the risk identified by the tribunal as justification for an interim order. In K v General Medical Council [2022] CSIH 44 the doctor was on an interim suspension order after he was arrested and charged with rape. He was acquitted and the order was changed to conditions, requiring him to notify the GMC of any new job. The GMC applied to the Court of Session for an extension of this order prior to its expiry. The court noted:

> "*The reasonable and properly informed member of the public would be aware that the allegation against the appellant has no connection to clinical practice and that the GMC has not sought to identify any clinical risk to the appellant's patients. He or she would be aware that the charge against the appellant has been the subject of a criminal trial and that the appellant has been acquitted by the verdict of a jury. He or she would be aware that the appellant is subject to an obligation to inform the GMC of details of his employment without the imposition of a condition to that effect, and it is not suggested that there is any history of non-compliance by the appellant with his obligations to the GMC. We note that he reported the charge against himself to the GMC.*
>
> ...
>
> *we find it difficult, in the absence of any connection between the allegation under investigation and the appellant's clinical practice, to see a rational connection between the conditions imposed and the reason for imposition of conditions, namely the public interest. The*

> *allegation under investigation is one of serious sexual misconduct outside the clinical context, and it has not been demonstrated that reporting and disclosure conditions related entirely to the appellant's clinical employment would address the concerns raised by that allegation in any way.*" [para 21, 24]

Proportionality

In determining whether to impose an order, and what type, the tribunal must consider proportionality. It must, therefore, balance the risk to the public or public interest as against the impact any order would have on the registrant, and others. Hardship from an order may take a number of forms. In Houshian v GMC [2012] EWHC 3458 (QB) King J stated the issue of proportionality

> "*cannot be overstated. A suspension has potentially three very important consequences for a practitioner. First there is the impact upon the person's right to earn a living: in this case the Applicant's pre-suspension salary was in the region of £150,000. Secondly, there is the obvious detriment to him in terms of his reputation. Thirdly it deprives the practitioner of showing that during the relevant period he has conducted himself well and competently and 'so as it were enhanced his prospects in front of the panel undertaking a final hearing' (per Davis J. in Sheikh at paragraph 18). I note that in Sandler Nicol J. agreed that 'the Panel must consider very carefully the proportionality of their measure (weighing the significance of any harm to the public interest in not suspending the doctor against the damage to him by preventing him from practising)'.*" [para 13]

It is common for the defence to submit evidence or make submissions regarding the financial position of the registrant in order to illustrate the likely adverse consequences of an order. It is also relevant if third parties will suffer if a registrant is prevented from working – e.g. children / family members who are being supported financially, potentially even patients.

Length of order

Most regulators allow tribunals to impose an interim order for up to 18 months. As discussed, any order must be proportionate – that applies to the length of order as much as the type of order. There should be no presumption in favour of an 18-month order. Harry v GMC [2012] EWHC 2762 (QB) noted:

> "*It should not be overlooked that Parliament has provided that 18 months is the maximum period of suspension that the Panel can impose. There will be many cases in which suspension is proportionate for a short period but not for as long as 18 months, given the very serious consequences it has upon the doctor concerned. 18 months should not become a default position.*" [para 18]

In reality, FTP investigations are so slow that an 18 month order is anything but unusual.

Review

Generally, regulators require interim orders to be reviewed every six months. Some regulators have provision for reviews to be conducted on the papers and by a chair sitting alone with the registrant's consent. Sometimes an early review may be requested, for example on the basis of new evidence.

A reviewing tribunal should consider the matter afresh – i.e. whether any grounds of an interim order have been met. It can revoke the order or impose conditions or a suspension in the same way as a tribunal hearing an application for a new interim order. A reviewing tribunal, however, may not shorten an order.

In practice any reviewing tribunals will ask itself "what has changed", and – in the absence of such a change – they are likely to maintain the order.

Challenging an interim order

Interim orders may be challenged in the High Court – e.g. under s. 41A(1) Medical Act 1983. This is not an "appeal", nor is the court confined to exercising a judicial review type jurisdiction. Rather, as Lindblom J observed in Abdullah v General Medical Council [2012] EWHC 2506 (Admin) at para 87:

> "*The scope of the court's jurisdiction under section 41A(10) of the 1983 Act is well established. The relevant jurisprudence is clear. In a case such as this the court is not constrained by the principles of public law that govern a claim for judicial review. I must decide whether the IOP were right to suspend the claimant while the allegations he faces are investigated. I must judge whether their decision was, and is, both justified and proportionate. Suspension will have been justified it was necessary as a means of protecting members of the public, or if it was otherwise in the public interest, or if it was in the interests of the claimant himself as a registered person. I must look at the IOP's determination and consider what weight I should give to it, remembering that Parliament has entrusted to them the power in the first instance to make decisions on a doctor's freedom to practise while his or her fitness to do so is investigated, that they bring to bear on this task their own experience and expertise and their own knowledge of the public's expectations of the medical profession, and that it is not their responsibility – or the court's – to make findings of fact or to resolve factual disputes.*"

In a similar vein, Cook v General Medical Council [2024] EWHC 1663 (Admin) summarised the approach taken to such challenges:

> "*the Tribunal's decision will remain intact and undisturbed unless the court determines that it is "wrong" (Sandler v GMC [2010] EWHC 1029 (Admin) at [12] , per Nicol J (" Sandler ")). Thus, this is not an unrestricted merits appeal since the task of this court is tempered by affording special weight to the decision of the Tribunal below.*

This is because the High Court has historically recognised that it is being asked to overturn the decision of a specialist disciplinary panel, which is ordinarily entitled to be afforded considerable respect (Harry v GMC [2012] EWHC 2762 (QB) at [2], per Burnett J (as he then was)). The test this court must apply may be formulated in different ways:

Whether the court should exercise its discretion ("may" vary/revoke) differently to the Tribunal, while affording the expert tribunal's decision due respect;

Or

Determining what is the "appropriate" order in the case, a matter for this court to determine itself on all the evidence now available to it, again respecting but not being subservient to the Tribunal's decision, and only disturbing it if it is wrong." [para 11-13]

In respect of new evidence, unlike a substantive appeal, there is not need to satisfy the strict admissibility requirements of Ladd v Marshall (discussed in the appeal section). Sandler v General Medical Council [2010] EWHC 1029 (Admin) commented:

"*My consideration of the application must surely start from the position that the IOP has thought that interim suspension is the right course... To describe the process as an 'appeal' may not do full justice to the power of the Court. It would seem to me that the Court does have power to consider subsequent developments and (where appropriate) fresh evidence. However, in my judgment the term does correctly acknowledge that in this context, unlike an application under s.41A(7), the Court is faced with an extant order of the IOP which it would only terminate if it thought that the order was wrong.*" [para 12]

There may be relevant additional evidence to be adduced, which was not available at the initial hearing. For example, evidence demonstrating the impact the order has had on the registrant concerned.

There is, however, a critical limitation to the High Court's powers when considering such a challenge. The court can remove a suspension or conditions order. It may amend conditions. It may shorten an order. However, it cannot substitute a suspension for conditions or vice versa.

If the court considers an interim suspension order is wrong, and conditions should have been imposed, it could leave the order intact and make pointed observations to this effect to assist the registrant at any review of the order. It could potentially remove the interim suspension order and leave it open to the regulator to apply for a new order.

Interim order extension

Most regulators may apply to the Hight Court for an interim order extension of up to 12 months at a time. The leading case is General Medical Council v Hiew [2007] EWCA Civ 369. Again, this commented that the powers to extend or shorten an order are "*original powers and not merely powers of judicial review*" [para 27]. The court should be guided by the same criteria relevant to imposing an interim order in the first place,

> "*namely the protection of the public, the public interest or the practitioner's own interests. This means… that the court can take into account such matters as the gravity of the allegations, the nature of the evidence, the seriousness of the risk of harm to patients, the reasons why the case has not been concluded and the prejudice to the practitioner if an interim order is continued. The onus of satisfying the court that the criteria are met falls on the GMC as the applicant for the extension under section 41A(7)*". [para 28]

The court will expect to see witness evidence from the regulator setting out the progress made on the case, why there has been delay, and on what basis the proposed extension is required.

CHAPTER FOUR

LEGAL ARGUMENTS

There are, of course, no limit to the kind of legal arguments which may arise in a regulatory case. I deal below with those I have come across.

Application for disclosure

Most regulatory FTP rules are silent on the issue of disclosure. In general terms, there are no reciprocal disclosure obligations on a registrant. Indeed, whilst regulators have powers to compel documentation, in general these do <u>not</u> apply to the registrant: s.35A Medical Act 1983 states:

> "*(1) For the purpose of assisting the General Council or any of their committees or the Registrar in carrying out functions in respect of a practitioner's fitness to practise, or for the purpose of assisting the Registrar in carrying out functions in respect of identifying any person registered by virtue of section 18A(1)(b)], a person authorised by the Council may require—*
>
> *(a) a practitioner (**except the practitioner in respect of whom the information or document is sought**); or*
>
> *(b) any other person, who in his opinion is able to supply information or produce any document which appears relevant to the discharge of any such function, to supply such information or produce such a document.*" [emphasis added]
>
> [See also s. 49 the Pharmacy Order 2010, s. 33B Dentist Act 1984, Article 25 Nursing and Midwifery Order 2001]

The interpretation of the same restriction in s.33B Dentists Act 1984 was considered in General Dental Council v Savery [2011] EWHC 3011 (Admin) where the court commented:

> "*I found it odd that section 33B(2) creates a power for the GDC to obtain relevant information and documents from any person other than the dentist whose fitness to practise is in question (i.e. the very person who might be thought to have the best information and documents relating to the allegation which falls to be examined).*" [para 37]

There remains a duty on the regulator to disclose material which undermines its case or supports the defence. A registrant is entitled in the ordinary way to any documents which might support his case or tend to undermine the regulator's case. This is a continuing obligation throughout the currency of the case.

Drafts of documents, for example witness statements, are potentially disclosable. In R (McCarthy) v Visitors of the Inns of Court [2013] EWHC 3253 (admin), the court considered the non-disclosure of a draft statement:

> "*it seems to me beyond question that in disciplinary proceedings with the potential for such grave consequences, draft statements capable of being used to discredit a witness should be disclosed… The demands of elementary fairness impose such an obligation.*" [para 17]

In addition to these disclosure obligations, in some circumstances a regulator may be under a duty to obtain evidence from a third party at the request of the defence. This duty was considered in R (Johnson and Maggs) v NMC [2008] EWHC 885 (admin). Essentially, it may arise if the regulator is in a better position than the registrant to obtain such evidence. The registrant should explain what they want, why it is relevant, and why they cannot obtain it themselves. Of course, this carries risks since the regulator will see the fruits of any such inquiries first.

Abuse of process

The caselaw surrounding such an application borrows heavily from criminal proceedings. It is generally accepted there is a general power for a regulatory tribunal to protect its process from abuse, although the rules are silent in the issue.

A stay may be granted where (i) the registrant cannot receive a fair trial, (ii) it would be unfair to try the registrant – meaning, "*it would offend the court's sense of justice and propriety to be asked to try the accused in the particular circumstances of the case*" or would "*undermine public confidence in the justice system and bring it into disrepute*". (R v Maxwell [2011] 1 WLR 1837, para 13). It is a remedy of last resort.

Most arguments in disciplinary cases are based on the argument the registrant cannot be tried fairly. Of course, the hearing process should be capable of addressing that unfairness – e.g. legal directions to ignore x or y, exclusion of evidence, an adjournment to enable an issue of non-disclosure to be resolved.

Delay may form the basis of an argument for abuse of process. Again, the threshold is high. Such a submission may be combined with the loss of evidence or the unavailability of witnesses caused by the delay. The court observed in R v Sawoniuk [2000] 2 Cr. App. R. 220, para 231 it was "*entirely speculative whether the unavailability of other witnesses represented a detriment to the appellant or a bonus*". In a regulatory context, however, it may well be that due to the passage of time a registrant will have properly and lawfully deleted the very records needed to be able to respond to a complaint. That loss of evidence could factor into an abuse argument.

Failures in the disclosure process could also amount to an abuse, but in most cases the unfairness can be cured by less extreme means. We have discussed these already.

The second limb identified in Maxwell is rarely employed. The bar is set extremely high. [Warren v Att.-Gen. for Jersey [2012] 1 A.C. 22, PC, applied in R (Clinton) v General Medical Council [2017] EWHC 3304 (Admin)].

Council for the Regulation of Health Care Professionals v General Medical Council and Saluja [2006] EWHC 2784 (Admin) is a rare case involving this second limb. The court considered to what extent a professional could argue entrapment by an undercover reporter. The doctor attempted to draw a parallel with police entrapment. The court summarised the position in regulatory proceedings in these terms:

> "*to impose a stay is exceptional… (T)he principle behind it is the court's repugnance in permitting its process to be used in the face of the executive's misuse of state power by its agents. To involve the court in convicting a defendant who has been the victim of such misuse of state power would compromise the integrity of the judicial system.*
>
> *… the position as far as misconduct of non-state agents is concerned, is wholly different. By definition no question arises in such a case of the state seeking to rely upon evidence which by its own misuse of power it has effectively created. The rationale of the doctrine of abuse of process is therefore absent. However, the authorities leave open the possibility of a successful application of a stay on the basis of entrapment by non state agents. The reasoning I take to be this: given sufficiently gross misconduct by the non-state agent, it would be an abuse of the court's process (and a breach of Article 6) for the state to seek to rely on the resulting evidence. In other words, so serious would the conduct of the non state agent have to be that reliance upon it in the court's proceedings would compromise the court's integrity.*" [para 79-81]

On the facts of the case, the court rejected the suggestion there was an abuse of process.

Particularising charges

A lack of particularisation may be raised as a preliminary legal point. In R (Johnson and Maggs) v Nursing and Midwifery Council [2008] EWHC 885 (Admin) analysed the issue in this way:

> "*Firstly, whether the challenges in the circumstances of the case provided sufficient information to enable those charged to know, with reasonable clarity, the case they have to meet. Secondly, whether they know enough about the charges to enable them to prepare their defences.*" [para 102]

By way of example, in R (Squier) v General Medical Council [2015] EWHC 299 (Admin), the GMC alleged the doctor had improperly cited certain research papers in support of their position "*including*" certain reports itemised in the charge. The word "*include*" was problematic:

> "*The word "including" however gives far too large a scope to the GMC to add other reports at any stage of its choosing. The reports relied on should all be particularised or the word "including" should be dropped.*" [para 54]

The issue of particularisation has often arisen in relation to the pleading of dishonesty. Such an allegation has to be set out clearly and explicitly. It is usually appropriate to particularise the knowledge / intention attributed to the registrant which makes the act dishonest.

In Fish v General Medical Council [2012] EWHC 1269 (Admin), the court noted that dishonesty should only be founded "*on solid grounds*". It can be easily alleged and is often difficult to defend. It went on:

> "*an allegation (a) that should not be made without good reason, (b) when it is made it should be clearly particularised so that the person against whom it is made knows how the allegation is put and (c) that when a hearing takes place at which the allegation is tested, the person against whom it is made should have the allegation fairly and*

> *squarely put to him so that he can seek to answer it… At the end of the day, no-one should be found to have been dishonest on a side wind or by some kind of default setting in the mechanism of the inquiry.*" [para 69]

By way of example, in Yassin v The General Medical Council [2015] EWHC 2955 (Admin) Dr Yassin faced an allegation that on unspecified dates over almost a year, when asked why outstanding jobs for patients had not been done, she dishonestly claimed that she did not know jobs needed doing, or she had not been given the task in question, or they had been completed. This lacked specificity:

> "*In particular, nothing was provided to explain how the inference of falsity could be drawn. In my view, without more specific allegations it was impossible for the appellant to respond properly to these charges and for the Panel to come to any conclusion about her state of mind at the time… It is not good enough to make a bald allegation as contained in this charge as a basis for a finding of dishonesty.*" [para 27]

In EQ v Disclosure and Barring Service [2025] UKUT 038 (AAC) the Upper Tribunal applied the same principles of particularisation as FTP proceedings. The DBS alleged EQ had made medication errors over two days whilst working at a care home. The DBS did not specify the medications in question, the patients involved or the number of errors. It provided documentation in support of its case, which included minutes of an investigative meeting at the Care Home, and the Home's referral to the DBS summarising its findings, but no medication administration records. This allegation was found proved. On appeal the DBS argued the underlying evidence made the basis of the allegation sufficiently clear. The Upper Tribunal disagreed.

> "*In our view, Mr Geering's submissions on this issue are well-founded. While we acknowledge the protective role the DBS has, its decisions in furtherance of that role may have draconian effects on those who lose their livelihood or at least their ability to engage in*

> *their chosen field in consequence. Although none of the authorities on which Mr Geering relies are strictly binding upon us, we respectfully agree with them…*
>
> *While we acknowledge the care with which Mr Webster as a professional advocate has pieced together information relating to some (though not completely in relation to all) of the allegations that could be derived from the material sent… we do not consider that that was a reasonable step to require of the person whose conduct was in issue…*
>
> *In our judgment, she is entitled to make her representations in response to a properly particularised… letter*" [para 56-60]

When making an argument regarding particularity, the solution will often be for the prosecution to amend its allegation to make the basis clearer. However, where the evidence does not allow for clearer particularisation, the allegation must fail.

Matters outside of the Notice of Hearing

The Notice of Hearing should set out the charges faced by the practitioner. It is on the basis of these particulars that the regulator seeks a finding of impairment. Where relevant, in addition to the matters pleaded in the Notice, it may be relevant to adduce the practitioner's fitness to practise history at the impairment or sanction stage.

However, it is ordinarily inappropriate to rely on other allegations – not included in the Notice – to justify a finding of impairment. As Collins J remarked in Roomi v GMC [2009] EWHC 2188 (Admin): "*it is perhaps self evident, that the practitioner faces an allegation which is contained in the notice and no other allegation*". [para 17]

It is far from unknown for a regulator to include reference to other allegations in the papers, which do not form part of the Notice of

Hearing. Such an approach is improper and other allegations should be redacted.

In Chauhan v General Medical Council [2010] EWHC 2093 (Admin) the tribunal went outside the charges set down. The High Court commented:

> "*what they were not entitled to do in my judgment was to make prejudicial findings* [on matters]... *which had never been the subject of a charge specified in the Notice of Hearing and then use those findings to inform their decision on those allegations which were the subject of a charge...*
>
> *for the Panel to use such a consideration in their determination of the express charges which the Appellant did face, is contrary to natural justice. As has been said on behalf of the Appellant, had such an allegation been expressed in the Notice of Hearing, it would have been open to the Appellant as part of his defence to call evidence from those responsible for training and assessing the Appellant in the course of his Specialist Registrar training, to rebut the allegation.*" [para 82-83]

In Strouthos v London Underground Limited, approved and applied in El Baroudy v GMC [2013] EWHC 2894 (Admin), the court said:

> "*It is a basic proposition, whether in criminal or disciplinary proceedings, that the charge against the defendant or the employee facing dismissal should be precisely framed, and that evidence should be confined to the particulars given in the charge...*
>
> *Where care has clearly been taken to frame a charge formally and put it formally to an employee, in my judgment, the normal result must be that it is only matters charged which can form the basis for a dismissal.*" [para 12]

In El Baroudy v GMC the registrant faced allegations relating to his failure to assess a patient being held in custody, who subsequently died. At the hearing the GMC argued that his actions had caused or contributed to the patient's death. This issue of causation had not been explicitly set out in the Notice of Hearing. On appeal, the court criticised this approach:

> "*Had the GMC wished to pursue those allegations, which would have been highly material, then in my judgment they should have been clearly stated in the charges and, in the absence of being stated, evidence directed to those issues should not have been led and the Panel should not in any way have based a judgment as to whether the fitness to practise was impaired or as to sanction on any question of causation, causation being defined as causing death or indeed causing the loss of any real chance of survival.*" [para 14]

This rule is not absolute. For example, there is scope of admitting uncharged allegations as bad character evidence. For example, this could be to prove a matter set out in the Notice of Hearing, or to rebut a false impression given by a registrant. This use of bad character evidence will be addressed below. Its use is rare.

Similar fact / Bad character evidence

Bad character evidence was deemed admissible in regulatory proceedings – e.g. Farriers Registration Council v Craig [2017] EWHC 707 (Admin), and Arowojolu v General Medical Council [2019] EWHC 3155 (Admin). Its use is, however, relatively rare.

Under most FTP rules, the admissibility of any evidence is subject to the requirements of relevance and fairness. In assessing these issues, assistance may be drawn from the Criminal Justice Act 2003.

In McLennan v General Medical Council [2020] CSIH 12 the court urged caution in adducing bad character evidence:

> "*As a generality, those pursuing disciplinary proceedings should not be permitted to introduce evidence of general bad character as an element in the proof of dishonesty on a specific occasion. They are not to be encouraged to in gather evidence of bad character either to refute the terms of references, which might be, or have been, produced, or as an attempt to undermine either credibility or reliability. If it were to be otherwise, tribunal hearings would be greatly prolonged, and the tribunal could be deflected from its purpose, by parties addressing matters of peripheral, if any, significance*". [para 80]

However, the observation in this case referred to "*general*" bad character being used to prove a specific allegation. This is materially different, for example, from using specific bad character evidence to show the registrant has done a similar act of misconduct in the past, and is therefore more likely to have repeated this behaviour in the instant case.

If the bad character evidence being relied on does not relate to a previous disciplinary finding, it rather begs the question why it does not itself form part of the Notice of Hearing. In addition, proving such bad character may well result in inappropriate satellite litigation and may fall to be excluded on that basis. [R v O'Dowd [2009] EWCA Crim 905]

The most common situation where the issue of bad character will apply will be when the tribunal has to consider the cross-admissibility of similar allegations which may mutually support one another. In PSA v GMC and Garrard [2025] EWHC 318 (Admin) particular sexual allegations were cross-admissible against each other on the basis that such evidence served to rebut coincidence. The court provided the following guidance:

> "*i) There are two primary grounds on which evidence may be cross-admissible. Namely, (a) where it may establish propensity to commit that kind of conduct and/or (b) where it may rebut coincidence (Freeman [2008] EWCA Crim 1863 at [14] and [15]).*
>
> *ii) The Tribunal will need to decide on which ground or grounds it is being asked to cross admit the evidence and advise itself*

accordingly, in terms that are relevant to and reflect the particular circumstances in which the questions of cross-admissibility arise (Brennand [2023] EWCA Crim 1384).

iii) The Tribunal will need to take care to distinguish clearly between the grounds and to not advise itself on the other ground if only one ground is applicable, in order to avoid confusion (Nicholson [2012] EWCA Crim 1568 and BQC [2021] EWCA Crim 1944).

iv) The Tribunal will need to consider whether the evidence in question is capable of being cross-admitted, by evaluating whether there is a sufficient connection and similarity between the facts of the allegations (Chopra [2006] EWCA Crim 2133).

v) Where the evidence is cross-admitted to prove propensity in a case involving two allegations, before attaching weight to the evidence the Tribunal will need to be satisfied to the required standard that the first allegation took place before relying on evidence in respect of the first allegation to deduce propensity from the second allegation (Adams [2019] EWCA Crim 1363 at [14] and R v Mitchell [2016] UKSC at [43])

vi) Where the evidence is admitted to rebut coincidence, before attaching weight to the evidence the Tribunal will need to advise itself that (a) it must exclude collusion or contamination as an explanation for the similarity of the complainants' evidence before it can assess the force of the argument that the allegations are unlikely to be the product of coincidence, (b) if collusion or contamination is excluded, considering the evidence as a whole, the fact of two patients making such allegations reduces the likelihood of there being an innocent explanation for them (R v H [2011] EWCA Crim 2344 at [24]) and (c) it is not necessary to find one allegation to be proved before relying upon the evidence in respect of that allegation in support of the other allegation concerning the other patient (Adams [2019] EWCA Crim 1363 at [15])." [para 47]

Good character

A registrant of good character is entitled to an appropriate direction at the facts stage. Such evidence is relevant both to credibility and propensity. In Donkin v Law Society [2007] EWHC 414 (Admin) the court noted:

> "*In my judgment the evidence of good character in this case was relevant to the issue of dishonesty. As in a criminal trial, it cannot afford a defence in itself. Moreover, the weight to be attached to it is in the last resort a matter for the Tribunal. In the present case, the reasons stated by the Tribunal do not disclose that it gave any consideration at all to this evidence in this context*" [para 25]

Wisson v Health Professions Council [2013] EWHC 1036 (Admin) added:

> "*Now, in the criminal context good character evidence is always put before a jury on the basis that it can be considered in two distinct ways.*
>
> *First, it goes to the credibility of the defendant and it is a matter that the jury and the Court is entitled to take into account in assessing his credibility, where there are, as there almost always will be before a jury, disputed issues of fact.*
>
> *Secondly, it can be used as an indication that it would be less likely for a defendant of good character to have committed the offence in question. That, in a sense overlaps with the credibility issue but it is dealt with in the standard direction given to juries as a further basis for taking into account good character evidence.*
>
> *As it seems to me, good character must always be likely to be relevant for the panel where there is a substantial issue of fact to be decided and where the credibility of the registrant in the evidence that he gives, is an issue and it can also go to whether it is likely that he did*

do what is alleged against him. Both aspects were prima facie material in relation to the findings that the panel had to make in the circumstances of this case." [para 41-44]

Some regulators have formed the view this character evidence is not relevant to allegations of a clinical nature, and only really applies to cases of dishonesty, sexual impropriety or similar cases of reprehensible behaviour. In my view that approach is wrong. Such an approach clashes with Wisson. In respect of propensity, a surgeon is less likely to have failed to conduct an operation inappropriately, if they can show they has performed 1000 such surgeries previously without issue. Moreover, if there is any actual dispute of fact, a registrant's credibility will be in issue, and evidence of good character is relevant in that respect.

McLennan v General Medical Council did question the use of such evidence:

> "*The inquiry by a Tribunal into an allegedly dishonest act or other misconduct will, or at least should, focus on the act itself. The Tribunal will look primarily at the evidence which bears directly on whether or not the act occurred. It is important for a Tribunal not to be deflected from that task by delving too deeply into an individual's professional or personal background. Although that individual may well be able to secure testimonials to his or her good character from amongst his or her close associates, it is unlikely that the opposing party, who is attempting to prove the allegation, will have either the time, resources or ability to delve into the individual's past in an attempt either simply to refute the terms of such references or to secure evidence of a less than perfect past… Although it may be legitimate to establish that an individual has no previous disciplinary record, since that is a matter which is usually readily ascertainable, there must be practical constraints on the extent to which a tribunal should otherwise permit evidence of either general good or bad character, when that character is not the gravamen of the complaint.*" [para 79]

This observation, however, is out of sync with the Donkin and Wisson and others. Whilst the primary focus of any case will be the act itself, in my view character evidence should not be limited in the manner suggested. It is, therefore, helpful to obtain a good body of character testimonials from witnesses who know the nature of the allegations in question.

Hearsay

In my experience, hearsay arguments probably constitute the most common form of legal argument.

Again, the admissibility of hearsay evidence will turn on relevance and fairness. The Court of Appeal in Ogbonna v Nursing and Midwifery Council [2010] EWCA Civ 1216 stated it was wrong to admit contentious hearsay evidence and deal with it only as a question of weight. The tribunal must determine first whether it was admissible at all.

R (Bonhoeffer) v General Medical Council [2011] EWHC 1585 (Admin) noted the protections due under Article 6 ECHR and how important the ability to cross-examine a witness can be:

> "[It is] *capable of being a very significant advantage. It enables the accuser to be probed on matters going to credit and his motives to be explored. It is no less axiomatic that in resolving direct conflicts of evidence as to whether misconduct occurred the impression made on the tribunal of fact by the protagonists on either side and by their demeanour when giving oral testimony is often capable of assuming great and sometimes critical importance.*" [para 45]

The court enumerated the following principles:

> *"i) Even in criminal proceedings the right conferred by Article 6(3)(d) to cross-examine is not absolute. It is subject to exceptions referable to the absence of the witness sought to be cross-examined,*

whether by reason of death, absence abroad or the impracticability of securing his attendance.

ii) In criminal proceedings there is no 'sole or decisive' rule prohibiting in all circumstances the admissibility of hearsay evidence where the evidence sought to be admitted is the sole or decisive evidence relied on against the defendant.

iii) In proceedings other than criminal proceedings there is no absolute entitlement to the right to cross-examine pursuant to Article 6(3)(d).

iv) However disciplinary proceedings against a professional man or woman, although not classified as criminal, may still bring into play some of the requirements of a fair trial spelt out in Article 6(2) and (3) including in particular the right to cross-examine witnesses whose evidence is relied on against them.

v) The issue of what is entailed by the requirement of a fair trial in disciplinary proceedings is one that must be considered in the round having regard to all relevant factors.

vi) Relevant factors to which particular weight should be attached in the ordinary course include the seriousness and nature of the allegations and the gravity of the adverse consequences to the accused party in the event of the allegations being found to be true. The principal driver of the reach of the rights which Article 6 confers is the gravity of the issue in the case rather than the case's classification as civil or criminal.

vii) The ultimate question is what protections are required for a fair trial. Broadly speaking, the more serious the allegation or charge, the more astute should the courts be to ensure that the trial process is a fair one.

> *viii) In disciplinary proceedings which raise serious charges amounting in effect to criminal offences which, if proved, are likely to have grave adverse effects on the career and reputation of the accused party, if reliance is sought to be placed on the evidence of an accuser between whom and the accused party there is an important conflict of evidence as to whether the misconduct alleged took place, there would, if that evidence constituted a critical part of the evidence against the accused party and if there were no problems associated with securing the attendance of the accuser, need to be compelling reasons why the requirement of fairness and the right to a fair hearing did not entitle the accused party to cross-examine the accuser."* [para 109]

Following on from Bonhoeffer Thorneycroft v Nursing and Midwifery Council [2014] EWHC 1566 (Admin) put the position in this way:

> "*For the purposes of this appeal, the relevant principles which emerge from the authorities are these:*
>
> *1.1. The admission of the statement of an absent witness should not be regarded as a routine matter. The FTP rules require the Panel to consider the issue of fairness before admitting the evidence.*
>
> *1.2. The fact that the absence of the witness can be reflected in the weight to be attached to their evidence is a factor to weigh in the balance, but it will not always be a sufficient answer to the objection to admissibility.*
>
> *1.3. The existence or otherwise of a good and cogent reason for the non-attendance of the witness is an important factor. However, the absence of a good reason does not automatically result in the exclusion of the evidence.*
>
> *1.4. Where such evidence is the sole or decisive evidence in relation to the charges, the decision whether or not to admit it requires the Panel to make a careful assessment, weighing up the competing*

factors. To do so, the Panel must consider the issues in the case, the other evidence which is to be called and the potential consequences of admitting the evidence. The Panel must be satisfied either that the evidence is demonstrably reliable, or alternatively that there will be some means of testing its reliability." [para 45]

In that case two witness statements were adduced as hearsay. The tribunal should have considered:

> "*(i) whether the statements were the sole or decisive evidence in support of the charges;*
>
> *(ii) the nature and extent of the challenge to the contents of the statements;*
>
> *(iii) whether there was any suggestion that the witness had reasons to fabricate their allegations;*
>
> *(iv) the seriousness of the charge, taking into account the impact which adverse findings might have on the Appellant's career;*
>
> *(v) whether there was a good reason for the non-attendance of the witnesses;*
>
> *(vi) whether the Respondent had taken reasonable steps to secure their attendance;*
>
> *(vii) the fact that the Appellant did not have prior notice that the witness statements were to be read.*" [para 56]

This is a helpful checklist of factors likely to be relevant to most hearsay applications.

In addition to these factors, in Karout v Nursing and Midwifery Council [2019] EWHC 28 (Admin) the court considered the nature of the hearsay evidence itself when deciding it should have been excluded. The evidence in that case were non-verbatim, unsigned telephone notes from patients who allegedly had not received their medication. The court observed:

> "*it was not even a case where reliance was placed on a properly recorded witness statement from any of these four patients. All four of them had declined to engage with the process. The hearsay evidence was the oral response which each of them purportedly made to an enquiry by Ms 3, or in the case of Patient F by Ms 1, over the telephone. There was no audio recording of the conversation. There was no precision in the noting of the conversation. Although Ms 3 spoke of a template, there was no "script" produced to show exactly what was to be said in each conversation to ensure consistency in the questions asked. Whatever contemporaneous note may have made of any of the conversations had not apparently been preserved, which was extremely poor practice. The sketchy composite audit schedule was the sole eventual product of the all important telephone calls.*
>
> *Second and equally important, even if the Panel could fairly and properly rely on the accuracy of what the Patient was reported as saying, the context of the telephone conversations was very different from the formal setting of a request for information which might be used in disciplinary proceedings with the career of a midwife at stake. Ms 3 described the approach as making "welfare calls"*." [para 129-130]

White and Turner v Nursing and Midwifery Council [2014] EWHC 520 (Admin) analysed the use made by a tribunal of anonymous hearsay. It noted that:

> "*In the context of disciplinary proceedings, it is difficult to conceive of circumstances in which the admission of potentially significant evidence about the attitude and conduct of a registrant which is both anonymous and hearsay will not infringe the requirement of fairness.*" [para 13]

However, it also made clear that admissibility of hearsay depends on the nature of evidence in question:

> "*As I hope is apparent from what I have stated nothing in the principles which must be applied prohibits the introduction and reliance on anonymous hearsay in all circumstances. In particular when the equivalent of business records in a hospital context are relied upon, for example a note of a patient's record about his or her condition, it may not always be possible to identify the author, but such evidence is plainly admissible under Rule 31(1) because it does not infringe the requirement of fairness. It is what it purports to be: a contemporaneous note by someone doing their job of something which is apparent to them at the time.*" [para 15]

Of note, business documents are likely to be admissible even in criminal proceedings, which has more stringent procedural safeguards – see s. 117 Criminal Justice Act 2003.

Adverse inferences – silence or failing to produce evidence

Until recently, most regulators did not seek an adverse inference if a registrant chose not to give evidence.

One exception is Ashiq v Bar Standards Board (Visitors to the Inns of Court Case No PC 2010/0185A) (27 March 2013). Mr Ashiq claimed he had written and sent a certain cheque, and he produced a photocopy to prove this. The prosecution and tribunal asked to see a copy of his cheque book to see the date of the cheques sent either side of the cheque in question. He refused. The tribunal drew an inference that such records would not support him, and that approach was upheld on appeal.

This decision was very much the exception. The seismic shift in approach came in R (Kuzmin) v General Medical Council [2019] EWHC 2129 (Admin). The registrant faced an accusation of dishonestly failing to tell his employer of his interim conditions. When he declined to give evidence, the GMC sought an adverse inference against him. The tribunal agreed and the registrant brought an interlocutory judicial review. In rejecting this challenge, the court observed that in civil proceedings courts have long been entitled to draw adverse inferences – e.g. Wisniewski v Central Manchester Health Authority [1998] PIQR P324. The registrant relied on the alleged quasi-criminal nature of disciplinary procedures to justify why this principle should not apply to regulatory proceedings. The court rejected this argument: these proceedings are not criminal and cannot benefit from that exception:

> "*Where a person has a case to answer, if he remains silent, then, as a matter of normal processes of reasoning and common sense, it may be reasonable to draw the inference that he is unable to answer that case in whole or in part. However, for criminal cases, the common law attached to the other rights of an accused person (including the right not to self-incriminate), the right not to have adverse inferences drawn from his silence which he had the right to maintain. That was an exception to the general rule that a fact-finder is entitled to draw inferences from facts he finds to be true, including adverse inferences from silence.*" [para 33]

In addition to this, the court noted it was in the public interest that a professional person should give an account of his actions. This was in keeping with the point highlighted in Adeogba that a professional was under a duty to engage with their regulator.

As to whether it is appropriate to draw such an inference, in general it will require:

> "*i) a prima facie case to answer has been established;*
>
> *ii) the individual has been given appropriate notice and an appropriate warning that, if he does not give evidence, then such an inference may be drawn; and an opportunity to explain why it would not be reasonable for him to give evidence and, if it is found that he has no reasonable explanation, an opportunity to give evidence;*

iii) there is no reasonable explanation for his not giving evidence; and

iv) there are no other circumstances in the particular case which would make it unfair to draw such an inference." [para 61]

If a case proceeds beyond half time, it is very rare not to call the registrant as a witness. However, it may be wise not to do so in certain health cases. If a diagnosis is in dispute, the issue will turn on the views of the relevant clinicians, and the registrant's evidence may well not make any real difference.

Amending an allegation

FTP rules generally contain an express provision for amending an allegation, as set out in the Notice of Hearing. This may be done after an application by the prosecution, or of the tribunal's own initiative, after it has sought submissions from the parties. The question comes down to fairness. Where the substance of the case remains unchanged, such an application is likely to succeed. The more notice the defence can be given of such an amendment the better.

Using findings of another court or regulatory body

FTP rules allow that a conviction will be taken to be conclusive evidence of the offence in question.

Achina v General Pharmaceutical Council [2021] EWHC 415 (Admin) considered the scope of this rule. The registrant was convicted of theft and sought to go behind findings made by the judge in the sentencing remarks. In the rules the certificate of conviction was admissible "*as conclusive proof of that conviction and the findings of fact on which it was based*". The court found the certificate of conviction was conclusive proof of "*not only the 'bare' facts to be found in the certificate of conviction, but also the broader factual matrix on which the convicted person has been sentenced*" [para 84]. The factual matrix in such a case is to be found in the sentencing remarks.

There is one limitation to using the findings of a criminal court as conclusive evidence. This relates to any conviction which received a conditional or absolute discharge. s. 82 Sentencing Act 2020 states:

> *"(2) The conviction of that offence is to be deemed not to be a conviction for any purpose other than the purposes of—*
>
> *(a) the proceedings in which the order is made, and*
>
> *(b) in the case of an order for conditional discharge, any subsequent proceedings which may be taken against the offender under Schedule 2.*
>
> ...
>
> *(4) Without prejudice to subsections (2) and (3), the offender's conviction is in any event to be disregarded for the purposes of any enactment or instrument which—*
>
> *(a) imposes any disqualification or disability upon convicted persons, or*
>
> *(b) authorises or requires the imposition of any such disqualification or disability."*

This prevents a regulator prosecuting a registrant for a conviction in such circumstances. The underlying conduct must be alleged to be misconduct instead. In such a circumstance the certificate of conviction cannot simply be relied on as conclusive evidence and potentially the registrant can try to "go behind" the facts upon which the conditional discharge was based. [See Wray v GOsC [2021] EWCA Civ 1940]

As for findings in civil courts, these are admissible but not determinative. In General Medical Council v Spackman [1943] A.C. 627 the court noted:

> *"It seems obvious ... that, while the council might well treat the conclusion reached in the courts as prima facie proof of the matter alleged, it must, when making "due inquiry" permit the doctor to challenge the correctness of the conclusion and to call evidence in support of his contention. The previous decision is not between the same parties. There is no question of estoppel or of res judicata ... The decree provides [the decree being a decree of divorce in that case] a strong prima facie case which throws a heavy burden on him who seeks to deny the charge, but the charge is not irrebuttable...*
>
> *The council is further entitled to attach to the conclusion of the Divorce Court all the weight that is due to the effect on a trained judicial specialist of sworn testimony given, subject to cross-examination, before a tribunal which can compel attendance of witnesses and production of documents, but all this does not exonerate the council from refusing to allow the accused to put before it relevant matter in support of his denial."* [para 635]

The relevance of such judgments was highlighted again in R (Squier) v General Medical Council [2015] EWHC 299 (Admin). The tribunal must not substitute their judgment for that of the judge who heard the civil claim, but nonetheless such evidence is relevant and admissible. This principle applies to coronial findings also – Towuaghantse v General Medical Council.

However, findings made by non-judicial bodies like an employer's internal disciplinary hearing have generally been considered inadmissible by regulators, unless potentially as background. In Enemuwe v Nursing and Midwifery Council [2013] EWHC 2081 (Admin), the High Court noted:

> *"in this sort of situation where there has been a prior investigation and prior findings by a local disciplinary or investigatory person or body, the findings of that person or body are not, and should not be, normally admissible in proceedings before the NMC, nor put before the Committee*

...

I perfectly appreciate that the background to many, if not all, investigations, and ultimately hearings, by Conduct and Competence Committees of the NMC is likely to include some complaint or allegation and some disciplinary or other investigation at the local level. Often a registrant may have been suspended or dismissed, and the Committee will need to be informed, and will be informed, of that fact.

But there is a world of difference between their knowing that there has been some investigation, and their actually paying regard to the factual outcome of the investigation in reaching their own findings and conclusions on disputed issues of fact.

At the risk of repetition... normally the findings of fact made at some earlier investigation by another panel or another person are not admissible in proceedings before this Committee." [para 38, 77–79]

No case to answer

Most FTP rules allow for a submission that there is no case to answer. Even if they do not, that silence should not bar such an application.

Usually, a submission will be in relation to one or more of the factual particulars. It is generally accepted the test in R v Galbraith [1981] 1WLR 1039 suitably adapted for regulatory hearings:

"*(1) If there is no evidence that the crime alleged has been committed by the defendant, there is no difficulty. The judge will of course stop the case. (2) The difficulty arises where there is some evidence but it is of a tenuous character, for example because of inherent weakness or vagueness or because it is inconsistent with other evidence. (a) Where the judge comes to the conclusion that the prosecution evidence, taken at its highest, is such that a jury properly directed could not properly convict upon it, it is his duty, upon a submission*

> *being made, to stop the case. (b) Where however the prosecution evidence is such that its strength or weakness depends on the view to be taken of a witness's reliability, or other matters which are generally speaking within the province of the jury and where on one possible view of the facts there is evidence upon which a jury could properly come to the conclusion that the defendant is guilty, then the judge should allow the matter to be tried by the jury. [...] There will always [...] be borderline cases. They can safely be left to the discretion of the judge.*" [para 1042]

If a half time application is rejected, only brief reasons should be given. In R (Sharaf) v GMC the legal assessor at first instance had said:

> "*if you allow this submission, you should give detailed reasons for doing so. If, however, you dismiss the application and the case proceeds, it is generally considered better to say as little as possible in case, in giving detailed reasons, you give some indication as to the way in which you are considering the evidence at this stage and it would be improper for you to do so.*" [para 26]

In the judicial review which followed the judge referred to this advice:

> "*True it is that the deliberation ruling from the panel was a short one but, given the guidance from the legal assessor as to the undesirability of giving detailed reasons, that is unsurprising. In my judgment it cannot reasonably be said that the panel did not carry out a proper evaluation of the submissions it had so recently heard and did not weigh up the evidence in the round that it had heard from Dr Sheppard in particular. I am not persuaded that the absence of any "scintilla" of evaluation of reliability in the panel's open reasoning means that there was no such evaluation in fact.*" [para 47]

In addition to challenging factual matters, there may also be scope for making an application that a particular is not capable of amounting to misconduct and / or there is no basis for a finding of impairment globally.

It is important to consider how the relevant rule is phrased for each regulator. In R (Husband) v GMC [2019] EWHC 2210 (Admin) the GDC conceded the tribunal had erred in stating a half time submission could not be made on the basis the charge was incapable of amounting to misconduct.

Reopening a decision

There have been instances where one party or another have attempted to re-open a decision which has been made against them. There is a conflict in the case law. In TZ v GMC [2015] EWHC 1001 (Admin) a judgment had been emailed to the parties in advance of being announced on the record. The court considered it was open to Dr TZ to make an application to adduce further evidence at that stage. Gilbart J commented: "*I agree that after the factual decision was announced, the Rules did not permit the admission of the evidence. It is of course right that a line must be drawn somewhere. That line is the announcement in Rule 17(2)(i)*". [para 82]

Nduka v GMC [2017] EWHC 1396 (Admin) echoes this. After the factual determination had been announced, Dr Nduka attempted to adduce further evidence in an attempt to invite the Tribunal to reverse its decision. Laing J commented:

> *"The Tribunal accepted the advice of the Legal Assessor and ruled that it had no power under the 2004 Rules to re-open the fact-finding stage after handing its decision, referring to TZ v General Medical Council [2015] EWHC 1001 (Admin) , per Gilbart J at [82]). The Tribunal had announced its findings of fact, the first stage under rule 17(2)(j) , and now had to move on to hear evidence and submissions on impairment of fitness to practise under rule 17(2)(k) . The Tribunal advised the Appellant that he could apply to adduce this further evidence at the impairment stage. In my judgment, the Tribunal correctly applied the 2004 Rules."* [para 48]

These cases put the position forcefully – once a decision is announced there is no power to reverse it absent an appeal. However, there is some authority the other way.

The power of a tribunal to reopen its own decision was considered in Akewushola v Secretary of State for the Home Department [2000] 1 WLR. The court noted:

> "*For my part I do not think that, slips apart, a statutory tribunal – in contrast to a superior court – ordinarily possesses any inherent power to rescind or review its own decisions. Except where the High Court's jurisdiction is unequivocally excluded by private legislation, it is there that the power of correction resides.*" [para 295]

This principle was watered down in R (Jenkinson) v NMC [2009] EWHC 1111 (Admin). The nurse in question was convicted of GBH and struck off. Years later the conviction was overturned. Her case came back before the Professional Conduct Committee where her representative invited the Committee to set aside the earlier order. It declined to do so for want of jurisdiction. This decision was challenged successfully before the High Court. Cranston J commented:

> "*The principle established by Sedley LJ recognises that ordinarily tribunals do not possess an inherent power. The word "ordinarily" indicates that in some circumstances that power exists… for example, there is an accidental mistake, or a judgment based on a fraud or a miscarriage of justice, it is possible for a tribunal to take remedial action.*" [para 26]

In R (on the application of B) v The Nursing and Midwifery Council [2012] EWCA 1264 (Admin) the court sought to limit the extent to which the NMC used Jenkinson to allow tribunals to reopen their decisions. In that case the Investigating Committee (the precursor to Case Examiners) decided nurse B had no case to answer on an allegation. The NMC subsequently invited the tribunal to change its decision on the basis – inter alia – it had applied the wrong test. Relying on

Jenkinson, the tribunal concluded there had been errors in its application of a legal test, and that those errors amounted to a slip or accidental error. Lang J concluded this was wrong:

> "... *the IC's first decision, though clumsily expressed, was a legitimate finding that there were systemic failures in the way in which the care home was run and therefore there was no realistic prospect of a finding of impairment of fitness to practise on the part of the Claimant. This was an exercise of judgment on the part of the panel. Although the exercise of judgment may have been flawed, it cannot properly be characterised as a 'slip' (as the second IC panel described it). In my judgment, slips are 'accidental errors which do not substantially affect the rights of the parties or the decision arrived at' (per Sedley LJ in Akewushola). Nor can it be characterised as a 'miscarriage of justice' or a decision which was so obviously mistaken that there is now 'no room for speculation or uncertainty' as to the appropriate outcome (as in Jenkinson).*" [para 38]

She concluded, "*In my judgment, the correct course is to follow Akewushola not Jenkinson.*"

Despite this view, further authorities have built on Jenkinson. Fajemisin v The General Dental Council [2013] EWHC 3501 (Admin) supports this broader power. Dr Fajemisin faced allegations of fraud. Prior to the hearing he was informed that the registrar had decided that his name would be removed from the Register because he had failed to complete the requisite CPD hours. Before his name was in fact removed, the Registrar changed his decision. Dr Fajemisin disputed he had the power to do so and argued at the hearing there was a lack of jurisdiction since he was no longer on the register. The tribunal rejected this argument and he reiterated it on appeal. In dismissing the appeal it commented:

> "*in addition to cases in which a public body can re-visit a previous decision under the equivalent of the slip rule, a public body can re-visit a decision which was made in ignorance of the true facts when the factual basis on which it had proceeded*

> *amounted to a fundamental mistake of fact... if the original decision could be changed if it had been brought about by fraud, such as the deliberate non-disclosure of relevant facts, why not for fundamental mistake? If "fraud unravels all", why should fundamental mistake not do so as well? The resulting harm would be no greater in one case than the other.*" [para 37]

In R (on the application of Chaudhuri) v General Medical Council [2015] EWHC 6621 (Admin) the Registrar revisited and revoked an earlier decision to close an FTP investigation. The court upheld this decision, commenting:

> "*In my view, the inherent jurisdiction of public bodies to revisit previous decisions is not limited simply to correcting slips or minor errors which do not substantially affect the rights of the parties or the decision taken; on the contrary, public bodies have the inherent or implied power themselves to revisit and revoke any decision vitiated by a fundamental mistake as to the underlying facts upon which the decision in question was predicated.*" [para 46]

In PSA v GPhC [2024] EWHC 3005 (Admin) the regulator informed the registrant in error that their case was closed, and then later sought to reopen proceedings. At the hearing the Committee held that the registrant had a legitimate expectation that, following the closure letter, no further action would be taken against him. The PSA appealed. The High Court concluded the regulator was entitled to resile from the closure letter, It had been based on a fundamental error of fact: "*The principle that public bodies have power to correct decisions which they have made based on a fundamental mistake of fact applies here: see Chaudhuri.*" [para 62]

The power for regulators, and their tribunals, to reopen decisions in limited circumstances appears from these cases to be relatively clear. However, in Juchi v Nursing and Midwifery Council [2024] EWHC 2825 (Admin) the court cast the issue into doubt again. During the hearing the tribunal was asked to reopen its factual decision on the basis of new evidence. It declined and the High Court endorsed that decision. In doing so the court drew a distinction between courts and administrative decisionmakers:

> *"I have stated that in any event I have difficulty with the suggestion that a tribunal's jurisdiction extends to a review or rectification of its own decision (other than where there is a slip) within the framework of a statutory disciplinary system. This statutory, carefully staged, disciplinary framework is different from governmental or local authority decision making where the opportunity for successive decision-making or reconsideration may well arise. In some cases, although not here, a disciplinary framework affords a statutory mechanism for reconsideration. A disciplinary fact-finding also seems to me to be a decision of a different character from a decision of, for example a Registrar, within a regulatory body. In my judgement extraordinary or non-usual powers do not exist because there is no implicit fundamental injustice that requires the implication into an inferior tribunal's given powers of the additional, significant power to recall and rescind a decision when a statutory right of appeal, or a constitutional right to apply for judicial review already exist. The implication in such a case is for convenience only: jurisdiction already exists elsewhere to right the wrong."* [para 50]

The decision continued:

> *"I respectfully agree with the analysis of each of the earlier cases considered by Lang J in B. I have expressed my views above that on proper analysis I doubt the existence of an implied jurisdiction in (certainly) a fact-finding tribunal of limited jurisdiction to receive later material once their fact-finding task is statutorily complete, and likewise (probably) in a non inter-partes tribunal context such as a Registrar's decision. It is the case that the latter*

> *class of decision-making is often subject to an express power of review in regulatory systems, when further material may be submitted in any event, however, a decision on that broader question is not necessary to dispose of this appeal".* [para 59]

The position is far from settled. However, it seems to me if there is a power for a tribunal to reopen its decision, that power is highly circumscribed. The fact new evidence is unearthed the day after a factual decision is handed down is very unlikely to justify such an application.

Closing a case

An investigation may identify that there is no basis to the allegations. Some regulators allow the case to be referred back to the Case Examiners for them to close it (GMC, GDC, GOC, for example).

Before the tribunal, there is no clear mechanism in FTP rules for a regulator to be able to offer no evidence. However, regulators have attempted to adopt a pragmatic approach where possible. This has to be done with care, however.

In PSA v NMC and X [2018] EWHC 70 (Admin) the Family Court had concluded that either X or her partner had injured the child, and both had failed to protect it. As part of its investigation the NMC made one ineffectual attempt to obtain evidence from the Family Court. It failed. Consequently, it made an application to offer no evidence. It invited the tribunal to exercise its discretion to depart from the standard procedure for such a hearing, and hear an application for no case to answer at the start of proceedings. The tribunal acceded to the application. It uncritically accepted the submission that it was disproportionate to apply to the Family Court for evidence and the allegation was found not proved.

On appeal, Laing J accepted that it must be open to the NMC to offer no evidence in rare cases. However, r 24(6) requires the NMC to open the case and r 24(7)-(8) permits an application of no case to answer only after the NMC has presented its evidence. A general discretion under r 24 to alter its procedure in an appropriate case does not give the NMC carte blanche to disregard these particular provisions and principles. She noted:

> *"it is especially important, if the NMC considers that it is appropriate to offer no evidence, that if fully opens the case, so that the Committee is able to make a decision, informed by a sufficient knowledge of the facts, whether it is appropriate for the NMC to offer no evidence, or whether it should require the NMC to reconsider that view and try to obtain more evidence".* [para 57]

In essence, it was for the tribunal to decide if a case should be dropped, not an NMC official. That had to be an informed decision.

CHAPTER FIVE

PARTICULAR ALLEGATIONS

I do not intend to set out all the allegations you may meet. I focus on the most common and the most serious, and set out the relevant tests.

Sexual / Sexually motivated

Any allegation that particular conduct was sexual must be specifically pleaded in the Notice of Hearing. It cannot be brought in as a side wind.

This is usually expressed by setting out what the conduct in question was, and then including a rider that such conduct was "*sexually motivated*". Basson v General Medical Council [2018] EWHC 505 (Admin) stated this term meant the *"conduct was done either in pursuit of sexual gratification or in pursuit of a future sexual relationship"*. [para 14]

Whilst this formulation has been criticised – for example, in GMC v Haris [2020] EWHC 2518 (Admin) – it continues to be applied across the healthcare sphere.

Motivation, as a state of mind, is a matter of inference and not direct evidence [PSA v GDC and Danial [2024] EWHC 2610 (Admin)]. It is important not to equate inappropriate conduct with sexually motivated conduct. A tribunal should, therefore, consider whether there could be any other explanation for inappropriate conduct before deciding on sexual motivation. [Arunkalaivanan v General Medical Council [2014] EWHC 873 (Admin)]

Sometimes allegations simply allege that x act was "*sexual*", rather than "*sexually motivated*". This can be considered with reference to s. 78 Sexual Offences Act 2003. An act is sexual if:

> "*a reasonable person would consider that—*
>
> *(a) whatever its circumstances or any person's purpose in relation to it, it is because of its nature sexual, or*
>
> *(b) because of its nature it may be sexual and because of its circumstances or the purpose of any person in relation to it (or both) it is sexual.*"

Dishonesty

In respect of an allegation of dishonesty, there is no distinction between the approach taken in the civil and criminal courts, and the regulatory sphere. In Ivey v Genting Casinos [2017] UKSC 67 the Supreme Court set out the test:

> "*When dishonesty is in question the fact-finding tribunal must first ascertain (subjectively) the actual state of the individual's knowledge or belief as to the facts. The reasonableness or otherwise of his belief is a matter of evidence (often in practice determinative) going to whether he held the belief, but it is not an additional requirement that his belief must be reasonable; the question is whether it is genuinely held. When once his actual state of mind as to knowledge or belief as to facts is established, the question whether his conduct was honest or dishonest is to be determined by the fact-finder by applying the (objective) standards of ordinary decent people. There is no requirement that the defendant must appreciate that what he has done is, by those standards, dishonest.*" [para 74]

As noted already, the allegation should plead the particular knowledge / intention relied on to prove the dishonesty.

Integrity

Integrity is now sometimes pleaded as an alternative to dishonesty in healthcare proceedings. Historically, it has been a more common feature of legal and financial regulation. In Solicitors Regulation Authority v Wingate and another; Malins v Solicitors Regulation Authority [2018] EWCA Civ 366 the court attempted to define what it means:

> "*In professional codes of conduct, the term "integrity" is a useful shorthand to express the higher standards which society expects from professional persons and which the professions expect from their own members… The underlying rationale is that the professions have a privileged and trusted role in society. In return they are required to live up to their own professional standards…*
>
> *Integrity connotes adherence to the ethical standards of one's own profession. That involves more than mere honesty. To take one example, a solicitor conducting negotiations or a barrister making submissions to a judge or arbitrator will take particular care not to mislead. Such a professional person is expected to be even more scrupulous about accuracy than a member of the general public in daily discourse…*
>
> *Obviously, neither courts nor professional tribunals must set unrealistically high standards, as was observed during argument. The duty of integrity does not require professional people to be paragons of virtue. In every instance, professional integrity is linked to the manner in which that particular profession professes to serve the public.*" [para 97-102]

There has to be a connection between the alleged lack of integrity and the profession. Beckwith v Solicitors Regulation Authority [2020] EWHC 3231 (Admin) noted three points arising from Wingate:

> "*The first is that in the context of the regulation of a profession there is an association between the notion of having integrity and*

> *adherence to the ethical standards of the profession. This is consistent with the ordinary meaning of the word, namely adherence to moral and ethical principles. The second is that on matters touching on their professional standing there is an expectation that professionals may be held to a higher standard than those that would apply to those outside the profession. The third is that a regulatory obligation to act with integrity "does not require professional people to be paragons of virtue.""*

It went on:

> "*These principles must guide the search for the content of the requirement to act with integrity, so far as it extends beyond an obligation to act honestly. We also consider it to be elementary that they must be applied within the context of the relevant statutory framework – i.e. the framework provided by rules made in exercise of the power at section 31 of the 1974 Act. Section 31 contains a power to make rules "for regulating in respect of any matter the professional practice, conduct, fitness to practise and discipline of solicitors", and to the extent that there are applicable ethical standards they must be found in or derived from those rules. In this case, the relevant rules are those in the Handbook, and in particular the 2011 Principles and the 2011 Code of Conduct.*" [para 30-31]

The concept of integrity cannot be free-standing. It had to be linked to the profession's standards:

> "*The Tribunal cannot and does not have liberty to act outside the rules made under section 31 of the 1974 Act. Those rules must be construed coherently; the standards that emerge must be sufficiently predictable. This approach to the meaning of the requirement to act with integrity facilitates a principled approach to the important point raised by the circumstances of this appeal: the extent to which it is legitimate for professional regulation to reach into personal lives of those who are regulated.*" [para 34]

In this case, the solicitor had had a drunken "*sexual encounter*" with a junior colleague. Whether this amounted to a lack of integrity had to be considered in the light of Chapter 11 of the Code of Conduct: "Relationships with Third Parties" which "*is the obligation, whether acting in a professional or personal capacity, not to take unfair advantage of others. The Tribunal's finding that the Appellant had not acted in abuse of his position of seniority or authority puts the present case outside that requirement.*" [para 36]

Health

A registrant may face a particular allegation that they suffer from a particular health condition. This part of the case will be considered in private. In such cases the regulator will have commissioned independent medical assessors to review the patient, and give a view both on diagnosis and impairment.

CHAPTER SIX

DECIDING THE FACTS

Burden and standard of proof

The burden is on the regulator at the factual stage. The standard is the civil standard. Depending on the case, it may be worth addressing the tribunal on the inherent unlikelihood of the registrant acting dishonestly / in a sexually motivated manner etc, and the need for more cogent evidence to satisfy them on the civil standard. However, this is not a legal gloss to the standard of proof. Byrne v GMC [2021] EWHC 2237 (Admin) commented at para 22:

> *"(1) There is only one civil standard of proof in all civil cases, and that is proof that the fact in issue more probably occurred than not.*
>
> *(2) There is no heightened civil standard of proof in particular classes of case. In particular, it is not correct that the more serious the nature of the allegation made, the higher the standard of proof required.*
>
> *(3) The inherent probability or improbability of an event is a matter which can be taken into account when weighing the probabilities and in deciding whether the event occurred. Where an event is inherently improbable, it may take better evidence to persuade the judge that it has happened. This goes to the quality of evidence.*
>
> *(4) However it does not follow, as a rule of law, that the more serious the allegation, the less likely it is to have occurred. So whilst the court may take account of inherent probabilities, there is no logical or necessary connection between seriousness and probability. Thus, it is not the case that "the more serious the allegation the more cogent the evidence need to prove it."*

It is not unknown for tribunals to misapply the burden of proof. In Alam v General Medical Council [2025] EWHC 2907 (Admin) the tribunal had to consider whether a doctor had made certain amendments honestly. It noted in respect of one patient "*it was prepared to give Dr Alam "the benefit of the doubt"*". The court observed, "*The reference to giving her the benefit of the doubt "on this occasion" strongly suggests that on other occasions when there was doubt, such benefit was not given. In my judgment that would be to reverse the burden of proof.*" [para 36 and 38]

Limits of demeanour

There are numerous authorities dealing with the approach to be taken to evidence of demeanour. I do not propose to rehearse them all here, but rather to consider how the issue has presented itself in FTP proceedings. I will, however, note the observations made by Leggatt LJ in R (SS) v Secretary of State for the Home Department [2018] EWCA Civ 1391:

> "*No doubt it is impossible, and perhaps undesirable, to ignore altogether the impression created by the demeanour of a witness giving evidence. But to attach any significant weight to such impressions in assessing credibility risks making judgments which at best have no rational basis and at worst reflect conscious or unconscious biases and prejudices. One of the most important qualities expected of a judge is that they will strive to avoid being influenced by personal biases and prejudices in their decision-making. That requires eschewing judgments based on the appearance of a witness or on their tone, manner or other aspects of their behaviour in answering questions. Rather than attempting to assess whether testimony is truthful from the manner in which it is given, the only objective and reliable approach is to focus on the content of the testimony and to consider whether it is consistent with other evidence (including evidence of what the witness has said on other occasions) and with known or probable facts.*" [para 41]

The High Court noted in Suddock v Nursing and Midwifery Council [2015] EWHC 3612 (Admin) noted:

> "*the way in which the witness's evidence fits with any non-contentious evidence or agreed facts, and with contemporaneous documents, and the inherent probabilities and improbabilities of his or her account of events, as well as consistencies and inconsistencies (both internally, and with the evidence of others) are likely to be far more reliable indicators of where the truth lies. The decision-maker should therefore test the evidence against those yardsticks so far as is possible, before adding demeanour into the equation.*" [para 59]

In Dutta v GMC [2020] EWHC 1974 (Admin) the tribunal had approached the central factual issue in dispute by starting with a general assessment of a witness's credibility. Their account was in fact uncorroborated and described events ten years earlier. Only then had the tribunal gone on to consider the significance of unchallenged contemporaneous documentation. The court found it an error of principle to ask "do we believe the witness" before considering the documents.

In Khan v GMC [2021] EWHC 374 (Admin) the registrant faced allegations of sexual misconduct. As with Dutta, the tribunal declared a witness to be "*credible and consistent*" before it considered any of the evidence she had given. Unsurprisingly, the tribunal went on to indicate it preferred her account to the registrant's. However, two other witnesses had flatly contradicted the witness's evidence. In addition, the tribunal reasons were based to a significant extent on the twin fallacies that "*the more confident another person is in their recollection, the more likely it is to be accurate*" and "*because a witness has confidence in his or her recollection and is honest, evidence based on that recollection provides any reliable guide to the truth*". The court stressed: "*Reliance on a witness's confident demeanour is a discredited method of judicial decision making*". [para 110]

In contrast to this, Byrne v GMC [2021] EWHC 2237 (Admin) was more sanguine about using demeanour evidence:

> "*First, the credibility of witnesses must take account of the unreliability of memory and should be considered and tested by*

> *reference to objective facts, and in particular as shown in contemporaneous documents. Where possible, factual findings should be based on objective facts as shown by contemporaneous documents: Dutta §§39 to 42 citing, in particular, Gestmin and Lachaux.*
>
> *Secondly, nevertheless, in assessing the reliability and credibility of witnesses, whilst there are different schools of thought, I consider that, if relevant, demeanour might in an appropriate case be a significant factor and the lower court is best placed to assess demeanour: Despite the doubts expressed in Dutta §42 and Khan §110, the balance of authority supports this view: Gupta §18 and Southall at §59.*
>
> *Thirdly, corroborating documentary evidence is not always required or indeed available. There may not be much or any such documentary evidence. In a case where the evidence consists of conflicting oral accounts, the court may properly place substantial reliance upon the oral evidence of the complainant (in preference to that of the defendant/appellant): Chyc at §23. There is no rule that corroboration of a patient complainant's evidence is required: see Muscat §83 and Mubarak §20.*
>
> *Fourthly, in a case where the complainant provides an oral account, and there is a flat denial from the other person concerned, and little or no independent evidence, it is commonplace for there to be inconsistency and confusion in some of the detail. Nevertheless the task of the court below is to consider whether the core allegations are true: Mubarak at §20."* [para 17-20]

It may be overstating it, then, to dismiss demeanour evidence entirely. There may sometimes be nothing else. However, the importance of contemporaneous documents is highlighted repeatedly.

The value of medical records

The observations in Onassis and Calogeropoulos v Vergottis [1968] 2 Lloyd's Rep 403 at para 431 were quoted and endorsed in Lachaux v

Lachaux [2017] 4 W.L.R. 57, and in Dutta. They are highly relevant in any healthcare case where the substance of the defence rests on a doctor's notes:

> "*Witnesses, especially those who are emotional, who think that they are morally in the right, tend very easily and unconsciously to conjure up a legal right that did not exist. It is a truism, often used in accident cases, that with every day that passes the memory becomes fainter and the imagination becomes more active. For that reason, a witness, however honest, rarely persuades a judge that his present recollection is preferable to that which was taken down in writing immediately after the accident occurred. Therefore, contemporary documents are always of the utmost importance.*"

This point may be reinforced by reference to further caselaw. In Synclair v East Lancashire Hospitals NHS Trust [2015] EWCA Civ 1283 the court said:

> "*Clinical records are made pursuant to a clear professional duty, serious failure in which could put at risk a practitioner's registration. Moreover, they are not compiled simply as a historical record, they fulfil an essential and ongoing purpose in informing the care and treatment of a patient. Contemporaneous records are for these reasons alone inherently likely to be accurate.*" [para 14]

HXC v Hind [2020] EWHC (QB) added:

> "*The court can and often will take a starting point, but no more than a starting point, that a contemporaneous entry made by a medical professional is likely to be a correct and accurate record of what was said and done at a consultation/examination.*" [para 137]

CHAPTER SEVEN

GROUNDS OF IMPAIRMENT AND CURRENT IMPAIRMENT

For most healthcare regulators, there are several routes to impairment / sanction set out in the relevant legislation. The factual particulars ultimately serve to establish one of these grounds for impairment. These are commonly misconduct, deficient professional performance, health and convictions. Whilst all factual matters must be proved by the regulator to the civil standard, the question of whether they amount to misconduct, justify a finding of impairment or require a sanction is a question of judgment, not proof.

Looking at these heads of impairment: unless the registrant was given a discharge, establishing a conviction is easy enough. However, the concepts of what may amount to misconduct or deficient professional performance are more nuanced.

Misconduct

Misconduct has to be serious. The regulator will usually illustrate the seriousness of the conduct by reference to various breaches of the relevant Code or Standards. However, not every such breach will amount to misconduct.

In Johnson and Maggs v NMC [2013] EWCA 2140 the court noted:

> *"It was common ground, and the Committee accepted, that simple negligence was not sufficient for this purpose and that 'gross professional negligence' or conduct that would be seen as 'deplorable' by fellow practitioners was required."* [para 79]

This is not a test, but it is one formulation which is helpful in setting out the high bar which must be reached. In Calhaem v General Medical Council [2007] EWHC 2606 the court said:

> *"(1) Mere negligence does not constitute "misconduct" within the meaning of section 35C(2)(a) of the Medical Act 1983. Nevertheless, and depending upon the circumstances, negligent acts or omissions which are particularly serious may amount to "misconduct".*
>
> *(2) A single negligent act or omission is less likely to cross the threshold of "misconduct" than multiple acts or omissions. Nevertheless, and depending upon the circumstances, a single negligent act or omission, if particularly grave, could be characterised as "misconduct"."* [para 39]

Meadow v GMC [2006] EWHC 146 (Admin) considered negligence must be "*of a high degree*" to cross the threshold [para 88].

In Shaw v GOsC [2015] EWHC 2721 (Admin) the judge noted the legislation drew a distinction between issues of misconduct, and lack of competence. It concluded that the former *"does entail conduct that, to some degree, is morally blameworthy and would convey a degree of opprobrium"*. [para 47]

The seriousness threshold cannot be taken too far. It must ultimately be possible for a tribunal to find a failing amounted to misconduct, but that it requires no greater sanction than a low-level disposal like a reprimand (GDC) or a caution (NMC). The threshold for misconduct cannot be so high that, upon it being reached, such sanction would always be insufficient to mark the gravity of such reprehensible misbehaviour.

Whether conduct is deplorable or carries moral opprobrium will require careful consideration of the context. In Hindmarch v NMC [2016] EWHC 2233 (Admin) a nurse performed a check on medication. Whilst doing so a patient got hold of a bottle of lorazepam and took an overdose. The tribunal considered this was misconduct. In light of the issues surrounding staff levels, pressure of work, poor procedures, poor facilities, and the fact this was a single instance of negligence in a long career, the court disagreed:

> *"While it was a duty which had to be taken seriously it is the sort of mistake which can occur with a moment's inattention ... In the present case, whilst there was a clear need for care in the whole process, it would be unfair, in my view, to say that a moment's inattention automatically means that a nurse is guilty of gross misconduct if a patient is placed at risk of serious harm as a consequence. In my judgment, the Panel were wrong to criticise this single omission in the long and unblemished career of this dedicated nurse as misconduct."* [para 37, 41]

The case illustrates the point that the seriousness of a mistake cannot just turn on the consequences or potential consequences of that mistake. Almost all decisions in healthcare can carry serious or fatal consequences. It is a factor – but it is not determinative.

Often the Notice of Hearing will allege multiple factual failings. Suppose these are all proved. The question arises whether it is permissible to add them together and say that cumulatively they amount to misconduct, or whether it is required that each failure meets the threshold of misconduct in its own right.

The Court of Appeal looked at this issue in Schodlok v General Medical Council [2015] EWCA Civ 769. This cast doubt on the appropriateness of cumulating allegations. The majority of the court expressed the following view by way of dicta:

> *"I do not think it was open to the Panel in this case to bring in findings of non-serious misconduct in relation to the treatment of staff apart from Mr Marshall to feed its finding that Dr Schodlok's fitness to practise was impaired...*

> *I do not think that we should opine on the theoretical possibility that, in a particular case on different facts, a series of non-serious misconduct findings could, taken together, be regarded as serious misconduct. For my part, I would not think that the possibility of taking such a course in a very unusual case on very unusual facts should be ruled out, but I would prefer to leave the argument for a case in which such facts were said to arise. In the normal case, I do not think that a few allegations of misconduct that are held individually not to be serious can or should be regarded collectively as serious misconduct.*" [para 62-63]

The minority view of Beatson LJ, which he described as being very tentative view, was that this may be possible.

This decision was considered in Ahmedsowida v General Medical Council [2021] EWHC 3466 (Admin). The tribunal had decided not to follow the majority view in Schodlok. This was strongly criticised on appeal:

> "*To those observations from the Court of Appeal, the tribunal might have shown greater respect than they did. Rightly, they did not attempt to decide the point left open by the Court of Appeal and no more will I. But it is clear that they did not properly understand Schodlok. There was no mention of Beatson LJ's view being tentative and very preliminary, as well as (in a minority) less sceptical than that of Vos LJ with whose judgment Moore-Bick LJ agreed.*
>
> *Nor was there any comparison with the factual position in Schodlok; nor any consideration of whether the facts were exceptional here. Nor did the tribunal consider properly whether the GMC had sought as part of its case to cumulate a large number of findings of non-serious misconduct so as to elevate the misconduct to the level of being serious. That was, it seems to me, not the GMC's case. The tribunal appeared to regard Beatson LJ's obiter observations as providing them with carte blanche to cumulate charges considered in clusters. That*

> *approach is not supported by Schodlok or any other authority cited to me*". [para 107-9]

Ahmedsowida did not decide that accumulation could never be appropriate but it adds weight to the dicta in Schodlok. The usual position, therefore, is that the tribunal must consider whether each factual particular is – in itself – sufficiently serious to amount to misconduct.

Incompetence / Deficient Professional Performance

This ground of impairment is far less common. In Calhaem the court observed:

> "*(3) "Deficient professional performance" within the meaning of 35C(2)(b) is conceptually separate both from negligence and from misconduct. It connotes a standard of professional performance which is unacceptably low and which (save in exceptional circumstances) has been demonstrated by reference to a fair sample of the doctor's work.*
>
> *(4) A single instance of negligent treatment, unless very serious indeed, would be unlikely to constitute "deficient professional performance"*." [para 39]

It is harder to establish than misconduct. Ordinarily there must be a fair sample of work. That is likely to require further investigative steps by a regulator, rather than just investigating the particular concerns referred to it. Consequently, regulators tend to plead cases as misconduct where possible.

In the case of the GMC the registrant may be required to undertake a performance assessment – that is a series of tests and patient simulations. Their performance will be assessed and collated into a report. This will form the basis of an allegation of x, y, z failings which then support the ground of Deficient Professional Performance. This all comes at a cost. As I say, it is relatively rare that the GMC will go down this road.

Current impairment

If the ground of impairment is made out, most regulators require the tribunal to go on to consider if the registrant is currently impaired as a result. This requires the tribunal to consider not only the circumstances of the allegations, but what has happened since. For example, a nurse may have made several medication errors, which amount to misconduct. If, in the interim, they have attended a number of courses, worked well under supervision, been assessed, and there has been no repetition since, all that evidence will be relevant to current impairment.

However, impairment is not limited simply to establishing if the registrant continues to present a risk to the public in the narrow sense of the term. The court in CHRE v NMC and Grant [2011] EWHC 927 (Admin) at para 76 adopted the approach to impairment offered by Dame Janet Smith in the Fifth Shipman Inquiry Report (2004, Paragraph 25.50). It considered the tribunal should ask itself whether its finding of facts show the registrant's fitness to practise is impaired in the sense that they acted and / or are liable in the future to act so as:

- To put a patient or patients at unwarranted risk of harm; and/or
- To bring the medical profession into disrepute; and/or
- To breach one of the fundamental tenets of the medical profession; and/or
- To act in a dishonest manner.

This is not a test, but rather sets out questions the tribunal should ask itself.

In assessing the degree of risk of repetition, and the need to protect the public, the tribunal will be assisted by evidence of insight, reflection and remediation. It will wish to have regard to the factors set out in Cohen v GMC [2008] EWHC 581 (Admin), namely whether: "*his or her conduct which led to the charge is easily remediable, second that it has been remedied and third that it is highly unlikely to be repeated.*" [para 65]

As discussed, it is in this connection that it is important to deploy evidence of retraining and current safe practice. This may include: reflections on the misconduct, courses completed, reflections on those courses, testimonials, assessments, a reading log. Attitudinal failings – e.g. dishonestly – are likely to be harder to remedy but not impossible.

Risk of repetition is only one consideration. Grant went on to add this additional guidance:

> "*In determining whether a practitioner's fitness to practise is impaired by reason of misconduct, the relevant panel should generally consider not only whether the practitioner continues to present a risk to members of the public in his or her current role, but also whether the need to uphold professional standards and public confidence in the profession would be undermined if a finding of impairment were not made in the particular circumstances.*" [para 74]

A practitioner will need to keep in mind this issue of public confidence. Often a practitioner will struggle to understand why they may be impaired, even when the conduct in question is not directly connected to their clinical practice or has been remediated.

This issue of public confidence will particularly be engaged when dealing with instances of dishonesty or sexual impropriety or serious criminality. Indeed, it may well be appropriate to concede impairment on the basis such a finding is necessary to maintain confidence in the profession. That in itself can help to show a degree of insight.

It is necessary not to take this caution too far. There are cases where instances of dishonesty ultimately have not required a finding of impairment. In Professional Standards Authority v Uppal [2015] EWHC 1304 (Admin) the PSA challenged a finding of no impairment in relation to an allegation of dishonesty by Dr Uppal. She was a GP trainee. The Practice received a complaint from a mother concerning the care her baby had received. In essence, she complained that Dr Uppal had not contacted her following her baby's admission to hospital. Dr Uppal initially lied and claimed she had. When it was observed the records could be checked, she admitted her lie. The PSA contended that – given the seriousness of dishonesty – such conduct will inevitably amount to impairment. The court rejected that proposition.

> "*even in cases of dishonesty, a separate assessment of impairment is required, and not every act of dishonesty results in impairment.....the Panel was correct to assess whether or not Dr Uppal's fitness to practise was currently impaired, having regard to her conduct since the misconduct occurred, as well as the nature and extent of her misconduct. Thus, her apology, insight and remediation were all relevant to that assessment, as was the extremely low risk of recurrence*" [para 27-29]

Ultimately, it considered a finding of no impairment was reasonable in the exceptional circumstances of this case and it dismissed the appeal. It noted:

> "*the Panel was entitled to conclude that patients and the public were not at risk. Professional standards have been upheld, and public confidence in the profession maintained, by the fact that Dr Uppal has undergone a rigorous disciplinary assessment of her fitness to practise, resulting in a finding of misconduct on her record, with the option of a warning, by way of sanction.*" [para 34]

In Professional Standards Authority v NMC [2017] CSIH 29 the Court of Sessions agreed with Uppal: dishonesty did not inevitably necessitate a finding of current impairment. The registrant had inadvertently made two errors in the administration of medications to patients, and had subsequently dishonestly attempted to conceal this. In light of the low risk of repetition, her insight, her previous character and the overall circumstances of the incident, the panel determined that a finding of current impairment was not required to uphold public confidence. In dismissing the PSA's appeal, the court stated:

> "*... given the whole circumstances, and for the reasons explained by it, we are of the view that the committee was entitled to conclude that, notwithstanding her admitted dishonesty, SM's fitness to practise was not impaired. ... We do not agree with the submission that a perceived need for a penalty means that a finding of current impairment must be made. Whether to make such a finding is a discrete exercise to be addressed on its merits. In any event, in the circumstances of the present case, we would echo the comments of the learned judge in Uppal to the effect that professional standards and public confidence have been upheld by a rigorous regulatory process which resulted in a finding of misconduct.*" [para 30]

This case is a helpful antidote to one observation in Grant where the court had observed that a finding of no impairment was equivalent to an acquittal. This overstates the position. A nurse who is found not impaired will have no formal restriction or warning placed on their registration. But there will still be a finding made in public that they have committed x or y failure, and this has resulted in a finding of misconduct. As per PSA v NMC, that in itself may uphold the reputation of the profession.

Insight

In assessing risk of repetition, and to a lesser extent the public interest, a registrant's insight is of central importance. If possible, reflections should demonstrate the registrant's ability to reflect on why an error occurred, and how to prevent it happening again. A reflective attitude is likely to go hand in hand with remorse and admissions to the allegations. However, these terms are not synonymous.

A denial of a charge which is then found proved undoubtedly makes it harder to show insight. In GMC v Khetyar [2018] EWHC 813 (Admin) at para 49 the court commented:

> *"insight requires that motivations and triggers be identified and understood, and if that is possible at all without there first being an acceptance that what happened did happen it will be very rare, and any assessment of ongoing risk must play close attention to the doctor's current understanding of and attitude towards what he has done."*

Where an allegation has been disputed and proved, it will help a registrant to show through their reflections that they understand the seriousness of the findings against them, and what those findings mean for the public interest. Engagement with the regulator, and respect of the regulatory process, also helps to show a degree of insight. In the same vein, targeted remediation will still be relevant. It shows an appropriate attitude.

The interplay between a denial of an allegation, and whether this positively aggravates a registrant's lack of insight, and therefore points to the need for a higher sanction, is considered in more detail in due course.

Health

In health cases the issue of the public interest is of far less relevance, in my view. If a patient is not a risk to the public, there is no public interest in a finding of impairment because they suffer / have suffered from a health condition. The case will stand or fall on public protection, and the risk of repetition.

As noted already, a health case will require the regulator to call medical assessors to give a diagnosis, and a prognosis. Impairment is not assessed simply by focusing on whether the health condition is cured. Many conditions will be chronic. Nor does it prove no impairment if the condition (e.g. alcohol dependency) is in remission. Certain conditions are prone to relapse. This risk has to form part of the judgment

[Brocklebank v GMC [2003] UKPC 57]. Impairment will, therefore, take into account the whole global picture of the health condition. What is the nature of the condition? Is it being treated? Is it chronic? Is it in remission? When was the relapse? What is the likelihood of relapse after x period of time? What is the registrant's level of insight?

Of these factors insight may often be determinative. In a health context this will include showing the registrant has an understanding of the nature of the illness, the triggers for relapse, the need for a support network, early warning signs of a likely relapse, what to do if there is a relapse etc. Engagement with treatment and medical testing is also crucial. A risk of relapse may be tied to issues of stress at work. Evidence that such stress has been negotiated without any further relapse will be important.

In alcohol and drug cases the regulator will usually commission hair and blood samples to show if the registrant has abstained from a particular substance. Tribunals attach significant weight to these. However, they should not be considered in isolation. It is not unknown for contamination to impact on these results. If necessary, it may be appropriate for the author of any tests to give evidence.

CHAPTER EIGHT

SANCTION / WARNING

Warning

Certain regulators – like the GMC – allow the Tribunal to consider issuing a warning, following a finding of no impairment. A warning will appear on the doctor's registration but there is no formal restriction.

Particular guidance covers this issue. Essentially, the question is whether public confidence requires the misconduct is marked in some way because there has been a significant departure from Good Medical Practice. The court considered Dr Uppal's dishonesty, for example, warranted a warning.

Sanction overview

The point of sanction is not to be punitive, although it may have this effect. Since sanction is not intended to be a mode of punishment, matters of personal mitigation will be of less significance than in criminal proceedings.

The panel will need to consider aggravating and mitigating features, and the weight attached to them. Essentially, aggravating and mitigating features have to be evaluated, and not merely listed – Arunachalam v General Medical Council [2018] EWHC 758 (Admin) para 64.

Sanction has to be proportionate – in other words the panel must adopt the least restrictive means necessary to protect the public and the public interest. However, as Bolton v Law Society [1994] 1 WLR 512 noted, ultimately "*The reputation of the profession is more important than the fortunes of any individual member. Membership of a profession brings many benefits, but that is a part of the price.*" [para 519]

In determining the appropriate level of sanction every regulator will have Sanctions Guidance. This has to be considered with care. It will often provide a steer towards a particular outcome [GMC v Khetyar [2018] EWHC 813 (Admin)]. Whilst it does not bind a tribunal's hands, any departure from it must be justified. However, the High Court in GMC v Gilbert [2025] EWHC 802 (Admin) observed of the guidance:

> "*is not to be read as though it were a statute. It lists certain factors which may indicate that erasure is appropriate. Nor does the guidance mandate a particular outcome, as any decision on sanction is necessarily fact specific. The Tribunal found that Mr. Gilbert's misconduct was serious and that it impaired his fitness to practice. It was then for the Tribunal to reach an evaluative decision as to what was necessary to protect the public.*" [para 109]

Each regulator has a different approach to sanction, and slightly different options available. The GMC rules, for example, do not allow for any kind of warning / caution / reprimand to be issued if a doctor is found to be impaired. The options are: conditions, suspension or erasure. By contrast, the NMC and GDC, for example, do permit a caution / reprimand to be issued, following a finding of impairment. Care must be taken to consider the particular regime in question.

Moreover, certain forms of impairment cannot be dealt with by way of strike off when a sanction is first imposed. Again, this differs according to different regimes. For the NMC, a finding of lack of competence or health cannot result in a strike off until the person has been on conditions / suspension for two years. Interim orders do not count. The GMC contains no equivalent restriction for Deficient Professional Performance. It cannot strike someone off for health, although in due course such a doctor could be indeterminately suspended.

Subject to these qualifications, the basic options for most regulators are as follows:

No order: it is not a given a sanction must be imposed, notwithstanding a finding of impairment. Not doing so is, however, exceptional.

Caution / Reprimand: this essentially means a sanction is recorded on the registrant's registration showing they have been issued a caution. However, they can continue to work without any other restriction.

Conditions: the registrant can continue to work but only if certain conditions are fulfilled. E.g. a degree of supervision is put in place. This order should be reviewed before it expires and may be replaced / extended.

Suspension: the registrant is effectively treated as not being on the register for the length of the suspension. Again, this will usually be reviewed.

Erasure / strike off: the registrant is removed from the register.

The tribunal should work up the list, from least restrictive to most restrictive. The guidance will indicate factors likely to point to a particular outcome. Again, evidence of insight, remorse, reflection, retraining, safe practice will all be relevant. Testimonials will often carry weight, if they are aware of the nature of the case against the registrant. Whilst not determinative, a tribunal will generally be unwilling to end the career of a registrant who is a valued and respected clinician.

The relevance of denials / being disbelieved

If a registrant denies an allegation, and it is found proved, does this mean they should face a harsher sanction? Unhelpfully, the answer is sometimes.

The caselaw has not developed in a particularly consistent way. In Misra v GMC [2003] UKPC 7 the GMC charged a doctor with additional allegations of dishonesty relating to his denial of the clinical allegations he faced. The court thought this "*unnecessary and oppressive*". It pointed out that if his denial was disbelieved then "*the Committee would have to consider his conduct … on the footing also that he had lied on oath*" [para 17]. This passage was subsequently interpreted as allowing a substantive tribunal to factor in denials in the hearing as an aggravating factor at sanction.

Also, in Nicholas-Pillai v GMC [2009] EWHC 1048 (Admin) the tribunal commented at the impairment stage that "*moreover, it considers that this dishonest conduct is compounded by the fact that you have given inconsistent and unreliable evidence at this hearing*", and at the sanction stage it added that he had also given misleading instructions to his solicitors [para 12]. Mitting J commented:

> "*In the ordinary case such as this, the attitude of the practitioner to the events which give rise to the specific allegations against him is, in principle, something which can be taken into account either in his favour or against him by the panel, both at the stage when it considers whether his fitness to practise is impaired, and at the stage of determining what sanction should be imposed upon him.*" [para 19]

However, in GMC v Awan [2020] EWHC 1553 (Admin) Mostyn J disagreed with this approach:

> "*It seems to me that an accused professional has the right to advance any defence he or she wishes and is entitled to a fair trial of that defence without facing the jeopardy, if the defence is disbelieved, of further charges or enhanced sanctions*". [para 38]

In Towuaghantse v GMC [2021] EWHC 681 (Admin) Dr Towuaghantse's insight was described as "*limited at best*", substantially based on the fact that he had contested the factual allegations. He was ultimately erased. In allowing the appeal, Mostyn J restated his position from Awan:

> "*in my judgment it is not procedurally fair for a registrant to face the risk of enhanced sanctions by virtue of having robustly defended allegations made against him before the MPT, or before another court*". [para 63]

However, he then qualified this principle. If the tribunal were to find "*blatant dishonesty or the deliberate misleading of the tribunal*" by the registrant that could be held against them. This would need a "*clear finding*" – more than simply rejecting the doctor's defence.

Sawati v GMC [2022] EWHC 283 (Admin) reviewed the caselaw and has provided the fullest analysis of how to approach this issue:

> "*Two important and fundamental public policy interests are in tension here. The first is the right to a fair trial for doctors facing charges involving dishonesty, with a proper opportunity to resist potentially career-ending allegations. The second is the necessity for protecting patients and the public, who place a huge amount of trust in doctors (as indeed they must), from practitioners on whose honesty and integrity they cannot rely. These principles may be simply stated. How the tension between them is resolved on the facts of individual cases may be difficult.*" [para 80]

Balancing these competing public interests is highly fact sensitive. The starting point is "*doctors are properly and fairly entitled to defend themselves.*" [para 109] The following factors may then be of assistance:

- The court drew a distinction between dishonesty as a primary or a secondary allegation – that is between conduct which is intrinsically dishonest, like fraud or forgery, and conduct which is capable of being performed honestly or dishonestly, like record keeping. A rejected defence is more likely to be relevant in the former case.

- What did the doctor positively deny? The court distinguished between denying primary facts – meaning what happened / what was said etc – and secondary facts based on an evaluation of primary facts. The court added, "*Resistance to the objectively verifiable is potentially more problematic behaviour (and more relevant to sanction) than insistence on an honest subjective perspective.*" [para 105] This distinction is not absolute, however. If a registrant denies an alleged state of mind with an unreasonable defence, that may be relevant to sanction.

- Is there other evidence of a lack of insight other than the rejected defence? The court noted, "*a rejected defence which on a fair analysis adds to an evidenced history of faulty understanding is more likely to be relevant fairly to sanction than one said to constitute such faulty understanding in and of itself.*" [para 106]

- The nature of the rejected defence is important. To say someone has not told the truth requires more than simply a failure to admit an allegation. e.g. was the defence a "*blatant and manufactured lie, a genuine act of dishonesty, deceit or misconduct in its own right? Did it wrongly implicate or blame others, or brand witnesses giving a different account as deluded or liars?*" [para 108]

The question is very much fact dependent. Clearly, it should not be assumed that denials of allegations aggravate a case and lead to enhanced sanctions. However, it may be appropriate in certain limited cases.

Criminal convictions

The interplay between a criminal sentence and a regulatory sanction is not straightforward. Not least, personal mitigation carries less weight in a regulatory context. As the court observed in Low v General Osteopathic

Council_[2007] EWHC 2839 (Admin) at para 20, the seriousness of a criminal offence as measured by the sentence imposed by the court is *"not necessarily a reliable guide to its gravity in terms of maintaining public confidence in a particular profession"*. For example, *"a relatively minor offence of financial dishonesty may well be considered to be of the utmost gravity by the Law Society when dealing with a solicitor who has care of his clients' funds"*.

Plainly there is some connection between sentence and sanction, however. In Council for the Regulation of Health Care Professionals v General Dental Council and Fleischmann [2005] EWHC 87 the registrant was sentenced to a three year community order. Before the GDC he received a suspension order. The High Court considered this outcome unduly lenient. It meant he would be able to return to practise

> *"before he had satisfied his sentence… before he had … paid his debt to society."*
>
> …
>
> *"I am satisfied that, as a general principle, where a practitioner has been convicted of a serious criminal offence or offences he should not be permitted to resume his practice until he has satisfactorily completed his sentence. Only circumstances which plainly justify a different course should permit otherwise. Such circumstances could arise in connection with a period of disqualification from driving or time allowed by the court for the payment of a fine. The rationale for the principle is not that it can serve to punish the practitioner whilst serving his sentence, but that good standing in a profession must be earned if the reputation of the profession is to be maintained."* [para 52, 54]

This decision – if followed too strictly – is liable to create absurdities. To take an example, if a doctor received a community order for three years, Fleischmann would suggest that no period of suspension would be sufficient. A suspension order could only last 12 months – and at its expiry or review the sentence would still be live. A suspension order cannot be imposed on the expectation that it will then be extended by a reviewing panel [Khan v GPhC [2016] UKSC 64]. Therefore, erasure would seem the appropriate course of action. However, if a doctor received a short custodial sentence for the same offence, Fleishmann would not preclude a suspension order. So a more serious sentence would enable a more lenient sanction. Clearly, that is nonsensical.

Fleischmann has to be treated with appropriate common sense. Helpfully PSA v GDC & Naveed Patel [2024] EWHC 243 (Admin) noted that Fleischmann "*cannot be applied as if it were a rule*" and both it and the GDC guidance based on it must "*bend to the overarching requirement to impose a sanction which is just, proportionate and only that which is necessary to maintain public confidence*". [para 19]

Dishonesty

Dishonesty is a challenging allegation to deal with at sanction. Numerous cases stress the seriousness which attaches to such a finding. For example, in Nicholas-Pillai v General Medical Council the court commented:

> "*These cases always result in the balancing of one public interest against another. In cases of actual proven dishonesty, the balance ordinarily can be expected to fall down on the side of maintaining public confidence in the profession by a severe sanction against the practitioner concerned. Indeed, that sanction will often and perfectly properly be the sanction of erasure, even in the case of a one-off instance of dishonesty.*" [para 27]

However, it is important to note it is not a single, amorphous concept. In the context of healthcare regulation, in Hassan v GOC [2013] EWHC 1887 (Admin), the High Court noted that the term dishonesty "*encompasses a very wide range of different facts and circumstances.*" [para 39] There is a spectrum. A panel must engage with the nature of the dishonesty and consider how serious it is – Lusinga v Nursing and Midwifery Council [2017] EWHC 1458 (admin).

There is certainly no presumption in favour of erasure. As noted already, there have been healthcare regulatory cases where dishonesty has not led to any sanction, or only to a warning (e.g. PSA v GMC and Uppal [2015] EWHC 1304 (Admin)) Usually, however, dishonesty will be serious and will result in erasure or suspension.

Dishonesty is often considered to be evidence of an attitudinal issue, and therefore harder to remediate. However, it is not impossible. Appropriate courses address issues of dishonesty and professionalism. A practitioner can reflect on the causes of the dishonesty, and how they rationalised their behaviour. They can show an understanding of the impact this may have on others, and the wider "ripple effect" on colleagues, Trusts and public confidence.

In most cases dishonesty will attract a sanction. However, it is far from unknown for such conduct to be dealt with by short suspension orders or cautions, rather than strike off / erasure.

Interim orders

If a registrant has been on an interim order, that may factor into the assessment of proportionality. Ujam v General Medical Council [2012] EWHC 683 (Admin) stated an interim order "*should be borne in mind as part of the background circumstances, but it would certainly be inappropriate to regard it as analogous to a period of imprisonment served while on remand*". [para 5]

Kamberova v Nursing and Midwifery Council [2016] EWHC 2955 (Admin) added:

> "*the Committee must take account of any interim order and its effect on the registrant in deciding whether any sanction was proportionate. This is no more than common fairness dictates. If proceedings are long delayed and a person is subject to suspension in the interim period, that period of suspension may affect the proportionality of the length of the subsequent period of suspension. Whether it has that*

effect is for the Committee to determine. If the appropriate sanction is one of striking off, then the fact that there has been an ISO may be of no relevant effect." [para 35]

CHAPTER NINE

AN IMMEDIATE ORDER / INTERIM ORDER TO COVER THE APPEAL PERIOD

Any sanction will come into effect only after the expiry of the appeal period (28 days), or the conclusion of an appeal if one is lodged. Given the regulator will not want the public to be exposed to risk during this time, it will usually apply for an interim order (e.g. NMC) or an immediate order (e.g. GMC) to cover this time period. This will then fall away at the end of the 28 days or at the end of an appeal.

To take an example: a nurse has made a series of medication errors, they are found to be impaired, and given a conditions order for eighteen months. The NMC will apply, therefore, for an interim order of conditions in the same terms to cover the appeal period. The nurse does appeal but, two months later, they withdrew the appeal. At that point the interim order ends, and the substantive order comes into effect.

Again, there are variations between regulators. However, the general position is an interim order or an immediate order may only be granted if such an order is necessary for public protection, otherwise in the public interest or otherwise in the registrant's interest. Just because a sanction has been imposed does not mean an interim / immediate order must follow. In reality, if the tribunal has found a risk to the public, and a risk of repetition, then an immediate order is bound to follow. However, in many cases an order of suspension may be imposed for conduct which has nothing to do with their clinical skills (e.g. dishonest billing), and where the registrant has shown insight and remorse. In such circumstances, it would be wrong for the registrant also be subject to an immediate order – there is no risk to the public and the reputation of the profession has been upheld by the substantive sanction.

There are relatively few cases on this issue. Ashton v General Medical Council [2013] EWHC 943 (Admin) concerned a doctor who failed to make an urgent referral. He was suspended for six months and an immediate order made. On that issue the court overturned the immediate order. The court went on:

> "*The public interest is broader than the need to protect members of the public. The panel appears to have regarded the public interest justification to have lain in the maintenance of public confidence in the medical profession and declaring and upholding proper standards of conduct and behaviour. While these are very important purposes that are closely related to the Panel's power to impose sanctions, it is again hard to see why public confidence would be eroded by permitting Dr Ashton to practise in a remote field of medicine during the relatively short appeal period; and the upholding of proper standards of conduct and behaviour may reasonably be said to have been achieved by the Panel's decision to impose the 6 months' suspension, without the need for an immediate suspension as well.*" [para 81]

Davey v General Dental Council [2015] 10 WLUK 213 concerned a dental technician who worked outside his scope of practise, and submitted falsified records to the GDC. He was suspended for 12 months and suspended with immediate effect. This latter order was overturned:

> "*I do not find it quite so easy to see why the public interest which had up until then allowed the Claimant to continue to practise (subject to restrictions and supervision) required that that should cease immediately, rather than continue for 28 days until the suspension took effect or, if appealed, until the appeal was heard. The only reason given was the gravity of the misconduct, but even though on any view what happened was serious, it was not explained how — and I am not persuaded that — the public interest was benefitted to any significant degree, to a test of desirability let alone necessity, by the imposition of the immediate order.*" [para 14]

CHAPTER TEN

REVIEW

Regulators' FTP rules will set out the mechanism for reviews of substantive sanctions. The tribunal will need to consider if the registrant is still impaired and, if so, what sanction is appropriate.

Abrahaem v General Medical Council [2008] EWHC) 183 (Admin) noted:

> *"the statutory context for the Rule relating to reviews must mean that the review has to consider whether all the concerns raised in the original finding of impairment through misconduct have been sufficiently addressed to the Panel's satisfaction. In practical terms there is a persuasive burden on the practitioner at a review to demonstrate that he or she has fully acknowledged why past professional performance was deficient and through insight, application, education, supervision or other achievement sufficiently addressed the past impairments."* [para 23]

This burden is likely to require such evidence as (i) reflections, (ii) retraining, (iii) references etc. It may be advisable for the registrant to give evidence. This is not an opportunity to dispute the facts previously found proved, but to demonstrate insight and reflections relating to those findings, and to show current safe practice if possible.

The powers open to a reviewing panel differ depending on the individual regulator. However, in general, a panel can remove the order immediately, allow it to lapse at the end of its term, extend the order, or replace it with a lesser or more serious order.

To take an example: a doctor is found to have made clinical misjudgements and acted dishonestly. They are suspended. A review takes place a year later. The doctor shows insight into their dishonesty but insufficient re-training concerning the clinical concerns. The decision is made to replace the order with conditions. A further review takes place six months later. The doctor has been able to work safely in that time and has done further training. The panel consider they are no longer impaired and the order is revoked.

CHAPTER ELEVEN

APPEALS

Appeals out of time

Check each regulator's Act but the general position is they allow an appeal to the High Court within 28 days of a sanction being imposed. They make no allowance for appeals to be heard out of time. The appeal must be lodged in time, subject only to a very narrow exception. In Adesina v NMC [2013] EWCA Civ 818 the court considered a narrow discretion had to be read into the Order for it to be compliant with the ECHR. The conclusion drew on the extradition case of Pomiechowski v Poland [2012] UKSC 20:

> "*In my judgment, this requires adoption of the same approach as that of Lord Mance in Pomiechowski. A discretion must only arise "in exceptional circumstances" and where the appellant "personally has done all he can to bring [the appeal] timeously" (paragraph 39). I do not believe that the discretion would arise save in a very small number of cases. Courts are experienced in exercising discretion on a basis of exceptionality*". [para 15]

The courts have taken a very strict approach to this. As an example, in Gyurkovits v General Dental Council [2013] EWHC 4507 (Admin) his appeal was lodged one day late and there was evidence the Appellant was unwell. This was not enough. Stewart J commented:

> "[there] *would have to be very strong medical evidence to show that he was not capable – or essentially capable – of dealing with things at all during the relevant period in late February and March 2013. That is, in any event, controverted by the fact that he did deal with matters, albeit a day late. I accept that he has had medical problems; I accept that they probably do – to some extent – affect his*

> *functioning. But he would have to show a great deal more than that. I was not persuaded, having heard from him, there was the remotest possibility of showing exceptional circumstances based on the medical evidence.*" [para 17]

Approach to appeals

On appeal the test under CPR 52 is whether the decision was wrong, or there was a serious procedural irregularity.

A registrant's appeal is by way of a re-hearing, but without live evidence ordinarily. The PSA, when it brings an appeal, will do so by way of a review. The GMC currently has a right of appeal, and again this will be by way of a review.

Terming this appeal a re-hearing or a review hearing makes little difference, in reality. The re-hearing does not, after all, involve the re-hearing of any evidence. It is decided on the papers. The tribunal's decision is still given significant respect (see below). Essentially, however, a review is more supervisory in nature – Sastry v GMC [2012] EWCA Civ 623, para 107-8. A review should be less willing to interfere in a decision made by a panel.

On any appeal, an appellate court should exercise particular restraint in interfering with the findings of fact, especially where the tribunal has reached those findings after seeing and evaluating the witnesses. A finding which is based on the reliability or credibility of a witness will be "*virtually unassailable*". [Southall v. General Medical Council [2010] EWCA Civ 407, para 47] This comment should not be read as meaning "*practically impossible*" – see Dutta para 22. However, it gives a flavour of the hurdle such appeals face.

Restraint is also needed in respect of the tribunal's evaluation of facts. The court will only interfere if that assessment "*fell outside the bounds of what the court or tribunal could properly and reasonably have decided*"

[Solicitors Regulation Authority v Good [2019] EWHC 817 (Admin), para 30].

Respect is due to the decisions of a specialist disciplinary tribunal, with "*particular force*" to its judgment on sanction [Fatnani and Raschid v. General Medical Council [2007] EWCA Civ 46]. The "specialism" of the tribunal partly underpins the deference owed to its decisions. However, the relevance of this "specialism" will depend on the nature of the case. General Medical Council v Jagjivan [2017] EWHC 1247 (Admin) summarised it in this way:

> *"there may be matters, such as dishonesty or sexual misconduct, where the court 'is likely to feel that it can assess what is needed to protect the public or maintain the reputation of the profession more easily for itself and thus attach less weight to the expertise of the Tribunal ...': see Council for the Regulation of Healthcare Professionals v GMC and Southall [2005] Lloyd's Rep Med 365 , para 11, and Khan's case, at para 36(c). As Lord Millett observed in Ghosh v General Medical Council [2001] 1 WLR 1915 , 1923G, the appellate court 'will afford an appropriate measure of respect of the judgment in the committee ... but the [appellate court] will not defer to the committee's judgment more than is warranted by the circumstances'."* [para 40]

However, there is another issue behind this deference. It is unlikely to be appropriate for an appeal court to interfere with a multi-factorial matter of judgment. As Lord Hoffmann in Biogen Inc v Medeva plc [1997] RPC 1 noted, "*Where the application of a legal standard such as negligence or obviousness involves no question of principle but is simply a matter of degree, an appellate court should be very cautious in differing from the judge's evaluation*". [para 45]

GMC v Bawa-garba [2018] EWCA Civ 1879 endorsed this observation. The court considered whether suspension was reasonably open to the tribunal. It commented:

> "*The decision of the Tribunal that suspension rather than erasure was an appropriate sanction for the failings of Dr Bawa-Garba, which led to her conviction for gross negligence manslaughter, was an evaluative decision based on many factors, a type of decision sometimes referred to as "a multi-factorial decision". This type of decision, a mixture of fact and law, has been described as "a kind of jury question" about which reasonable people may reasonably disagree… It has been repeatedly stated in cases at the highest level that there is limited scope for an appellate court to overturn such a decision.*" [para 61]

The court went on:

> "*That general caution applies with particular force in the case of a specialist adjudicative body, such as the Tribunal in the present case, which (depending on the matter in issue) usually has greater experience in the field in which it operates than the courts… An appeal court should only interfere with such an evaluative decision if (1) there was an error of principle in carrying out the evaluation, or (2) for any other reason, the evaluation was wrong, that is to say it was an evaluative decision which fell outside the bounds of what the adjudicative body could properly and reasonably decide.*" [para 67]

New evidence on appeal

CPR 52.11(2) notes that "*unless it orders otherwise, the appeal court will not receive – … (b) evidence which was not before the lower court.*" Prior to the inception of the CPR, the test for the admission of new evidence was set out in Ladd v Marshall [1954] 1 W.L.R. 1489:

> "*first, it must be shown that the evidence could not have been obtained with reasonable diligence for use at the trial; secondly, the evidence must be such that, if given, it would probably have an important influence on the result of the case, though it need not be decisive; thirdly, the evidence must be such as is presumably to be*

> *believed, or in other words, it must be apparently credible, though it need not be incontrovertible.*" [para 1491]

These questions are no longer determinative but are highly relevant. Hertfordshire Investments Ltd v Bubb [2000] 1 W.L.R 2318, the Court of Appeal said these questions must be considered. It went on:

> "*There are, of course, strong reasons for this approach which has a long pedigree. It is in the interests of every litigant and the system as a whole that there should be an end to litigation. People should put their full case before the court at trial and should not be allowed to have a second bite at the cherry without a very good reason indeed.*" [para 25]

In practice, is it highly unlikely new evidence will be admitted on an appeal unless this test is satisfied.

Disposal

On appeal the court may either substitute its own finding / decision for that of the tribunal's, or it may quash a finding and remit the matter back to a panel to decide the matter again. Usually, this would be a new panel.

PSA appeals / regulator appeals

The PSA may bring an appeal under s. 29(4) of the National Health Service Reform and Health Care Professions Act 2002 if it considers that a relevant decision was "*not sufficient (whether as to a finding or a penalty or both) for the protection of the public*". s. 29(4A) provides that this question involves consideration of whether it is sufficient (a) to protect the public; (b) to maintain public confidence in the profession; and (c) to maintain proper professional standards. Such an appeal must be brought within 40 days of the end of the registrant's appeal period, or – if there is no right to appeal (because they were acquitted, for example) within 56 days.

Under s. 29(8) of the 2002 Act the court hearing such an appeal may substitute its own decision or remit the matter back with appropriate directions.

An appeal may be brought on a number of bases if it may have led to an outcome which was insufficient to protect the public. For example:

- The failure to call certain evidence, or exclude certain evidence;
- The failure to amend an allegation;
- The failure to put additional allegations to the registrant (under-prosecuting);
- The failure to find a fact proved;
- The failure to find an allegation constituted misconduct;
- The failure to find current impairment;
- The failure to impose a particular sanction, or include a review;
- The failure to provide sufficient reasons so it is not possible to determine if the outcome was sufficient to protect the public.

Such appeals are relatively rare. Currently the GMC also has a power to appeal decisions under s. 40A Medical Act 1983. This power is due to be removed.

MORE BOOKS BY LAW BRIEF PUBLISHING

A selection of our other titles available now:-

'A Practical Guide to Probation Breaches and Other Applications' by Mark Thomas
'A Practical Guide to Remarriage and Divorce' by Cordelia Williams & Claire Howard
'A Practical Guide to Privacy, Transparency, Reporting Restrictions and Closed Proceedings in the Court of Protection' by Laura Mannering
'Beaumont on Barristers – A Guide to Defending Disciplinary Proceedings (Second Edition)' by Marc Beaumont
'A Practical Guide to Payments for Environmental Services' by Ben Sharples
'A Practical Guide to the Law of Pregnancy and Maternity at Work' by Rebecca Thomas
'A Practical Guide to Redundancy – Second Edition' by Philip Hyland & Collette Moore
'A Practical Guide to International Issues for Scottish Family Lawyers' by Susie Mountain, Donna McKay, Ken MacDonald
'A Practical Guide to the Law on Deprivation of Liberty' by Ben Troke
'A Practical Guide to Rights over Airspace and Subsoil – Second Edition' by Daniel Gatty
'A Practical Guide to the Law in Relation to Inquests' by Ramya Nagesh
'A Practical Guide to the Construction and Rectification of Wills and Trust Instruments (Second Edition)' by Edward Hewitt
'A Practical Guide to Data Protection in Social Housing' by Clare Paterson
'A Practical Guide to Spousal Maintenance – Second Edition' by Liz Cowell
'A Practical Guide to International Parental Child Abduction Law (England and Wales)' by Dr Onyója Momoh
'A Practical Guide to Deprivation of British Citizenship' by Sean Ell
'A Practical Guide to Commercial Property Service Charges' by Rachel Garton
'A Practical Guide to Clinical Negligence – Third Edition' by Geoffrey Simpson-Scott (Geoff)
'A Practical Guide to the Rights of Grandparents in Children Proceedings – Second Edition' by Stuart Barlow

'The Electronic Communications Code: A Practical Guide – Second Edition' by Kerry Bretherton KC, James Castle, Mark Loveday
'A Practical Guide to the Independent School Standards – September 2023 Edition' by Sarah McKimm
'A Practical Guide to Estate Administration and Crypto Assets' by Richard Marshall
'A Practical Guide to Parental Alienation in Private and Public Law Children Cases' by Sam King QC & Frankie Shama
'Contested Heritage – Removing Art from Land and Historic Buildings' by Richard Harwood QC, Catherine Dobson, David Sawtell
'The Limits of Separate Legal Personality: When Those Running a Company Can Be Held Personally Liable for Losses Caused to Third Parties Outside of the Company' by Dr Mike Wilkinson
'A Practical Guide to Transgender Law' by Robin Moira White & Nicola Newbegin
'A Practical Guide to 'Stranded Spouses' in Family Law' by Mani Singh Basi
'A Practical Guide to Residential Freehold Conveyancing' by Lorraine Richardson
'A Practical Guide to Pensions on Divorce for Lawyers' by Bryan Scant
'A Practical Guide to Challenging Sham Marriage Allegations in Immigration Law' by Priya Solanki
'A Practical Guide to Digital Communications Evidence in Criminal Law' by Sam Willis
'A Practical Guide to Legal Rights in Scotland' by Sarah-Jane Macdonald
'A Practical Guide to New Build Conveyancing' by Paul Sams & Rebecca East
'A Practical Guide to Inherited Wealth on Divorce' by Hayley Trim
'A Practical Guide to Practice Direction 12J and Domestic Abuse in Private Law Children Proceedings' by Rebecca Cross & Malvika Jaganmohan
'A Practical Guide to Confiscation and Restraint' by Narita Bahra QC, John Carl Townsend, David Winch
'A Practical Guide to the Law of Forests in Scotland' by Philip Buchan
'A Practical Guide to Health and Medical Cases in Immigration Law' by Rebecca Chapman & Miranda Butler
'A Practical Guide to Bad Character Evidence for Criminal Practitioners by Aparna Rao
'A Practical Guide to Extradition Law post-Brexit' by Myles Grandison et al
'A Practical Guide to Hoarding and Mental Health for Housing Lawyers' by Rachel Coyle

'Stephens on Contractual Indemnities' by Richard Stephens
'A Practical Guide to the EU Succession Regulation' by Richard Frimston
'A Practical Guide to Solicitor and Client Costs – Second Edition' by Robin Dunne
'Constructive Dismissal – Practice Pointers and Principles' by Benjimin Burgher
'A Practical Guide to Religion and Belief Discrimination Claims in the Workplace' by Kashif Ali
'A Practical Guide to the Law of Medical Treatment Decisions' by Ben Troke
'Fundamental Dishonesty and QOCS in Personal Injury Proceedings: Law and Practice' by Jake Rowley
'A Practical Guide to the Law in Relation to School Exclusions' by Charlotte Hadfield & Alice de Coverley
'A Practical Guide to Divorce for the Silver Separators' by Karin Walker
'The Right to be Forgotten – The Law and Practical Issues' by Melissa Stock
'A Practical Guide to Planning Law and Rights of Way in National Parks, the Broads and AONBs' by James Maurici QC, James Neill et al
'A Practical Guide to Election Law' by Tom Tabori
'A Practical Guide to the Law in Relation to Surrogacy' by Andrew Powell
'A Practical Guide to Claims Arising from Fatal Accidents – Second Edition' by James Patience
'A Practical Guide to Asbestos Claims' by Jonathan Owen & Gareth McAloon
'A Practical Guide to Stamp Duty Land Tax in England and Northern Ireland' by Suzanne O'Hara
'A Practical Guide to the Law of Farming Partnerships' by Philip Whitcomb
'A Practical Guide to the Law of Unlawful Eviction and Harassment – Second Edition' by Stephanie Lovegrove
'A Practical Guide to Costs in Personal Injury Claims – Second Edition' by Matthew Hoe
'A Practical Guide to the General Data Protection Regulation (GDPR) – Second Edition' by Keith Markham
'A Practical Guide to Working with Litigants in Person and McKenzie Friends in Family Cases' by Stuart Barlow
'Protecting Unregistered Brands: A Practical Guide to the Law of Passing Off' by Lorna Brazell
'A Practical Guide to Secondary Liability and Joint Enterprise Post-Jogee' by Joanne Cecil & James Mehigan

'A Practical Guide to the Pre-Action RTA Claims Protocol for Personal Injury Lawyers' by Antonia Ford

'A Practical Guide to Neighbour Disputes and the Law' by Alexander Walsh

'A Practical Guide to Coercive Control for Legal Practitioners and Victims' by Rachel Horman

'A Practical Guide to the Law of Driverless Cars – Second Edition'

by Alex Glassbrook, Emma Northey & Scarlett Milligan

'A Practical Guide to TOLATA Claims' by Greg Williams

'A Practical Guide to Elderly Law – Second Edition' by Justin Patten

'A Practical Guide to Responding to Housing Disrepair and Unfitness Claims' by Iain Wightwick

'A Practical Guide to the Law of Bullying and Harassment in the Workplace' by Philip Hyland

'How to Be a Freelance Solicitor: A Practical Guide to the SRA-Regulated Freelance Solicitor Model' by Paul Bennett

'A Practical Guide to Prison Injury Claims' by Malcolm Johnson

'A Practical Guide to Advising Clients at the Police Station' by Colin Stephen McKeown-Beaumont

'A Practical Guide to Antisocial Behaviour Injunctions – Second Edition' by Iain Wightwick

'Practical Mediation: A Guide for Mediators, Advocates, Advisers, Lawyers, and Students in Civil, Commercial, Business, Property, Workplace, and Employment Cases' by Jonathan Dingle with John Sephton

'The Mini-Pupillage Workbook' by David Boyle

'A Practical Guide to Crofting Law' by Brian Inkster

'A Practical Guide to the Law of Domain Names and Cybersquatting' by Andrew Clemson

'A Practical Guide to the Law of Gender Pay Gap Reporting' by Harini Iyengar

'NHS Whistleblowing and the Law' by Joseph England

'Employment Law and the Gig Economy' by Nigel Mackay & Annie Powell

'A Practical Guide to Noise Induced Hearing Loss (NIHL) Claims' by Andrew Mckie, Ian Skeate, Gareth McAloon

'An Introduction to Beauty Negligence Claims – A Practical Guide for the Personal Injury Practitioner' by Greg Almond

'Intercompany Agreements for Transfer Pricing Compliance' by Paul Sutton

'Zen and the Art of Mediation' by Martin Plowman

'A Practical Guide to Adoption for Family Lawyers' by Graham Pegg

'A Practical Guide to Industrial Disease Claims' by Andrew Mckie & Ian Skeate
'A Practical Guide to Conducting a Sheriff Court Proof' by Andrew Stevenson
'A Practical Guide to Vicarious Liability' by Mariel Irvine
'A Practical Guide to Applications for Landlord's Consent and Variation of Leases' by Mark Shelton
'A Practical Guide to Relief from Sanctions Post-Mitchell and Denton' by Peter Causton
'A Practical Guide to Equity Release for Advisors' by Paul Sams
'A Practical Guide to Financial Services Claims' by Chris Hegarty
'A Practical Guide to Financial Ombudsman Service Claims' by Adam Temple & Robert Scrivenor
'A Practical Guide to Running Housing Disrepair and Cavity Wall Claims – Second Edition' by Andrew Mckie & Ian Skeate
'A Practical Guide to Holiday Sickness Claims – Second Edition' by Andrew Mckie & Ian Skeate
'Arguments and Tactics for Personal Injury and Clinical Negligence Claims' by Dorian Williams
'A Practical Guide to Drone Law' by Rufus Ballaster, Andrew Firman, Eleanor Clot
'On Experts: CPR35 for Lawyers and Experts' by David Boyle
'An Introduction to Personal Injury Law' by David Boyle

These books and more are available to order online direct from the publisher at www.lawbriefpublishing.com, where you can also read free sample chapters. For any queries, call us on 0844 587 2383 or email us at mail@lawbriefpublishing.com.

Our books are all generally in stock at www.amazon.co.uk with free next day delivery for Prime members, and at good legal bookshops such as Wildy & Sons.

We are regularly launching new books in our series of practical day-to-day practitioners' guides. Visit our website and join our free newsletter to be kept informed and to receive special offers, free chapters, etc.

You can also follow us on Twitter at www.twitter.com/lawbriefpub.

www.ingramcontent.com/pod-product-compliance
Lightning Source LLC
LaVergne TN
LVHW022102200926
848481LV00003B/1042
9781918241297